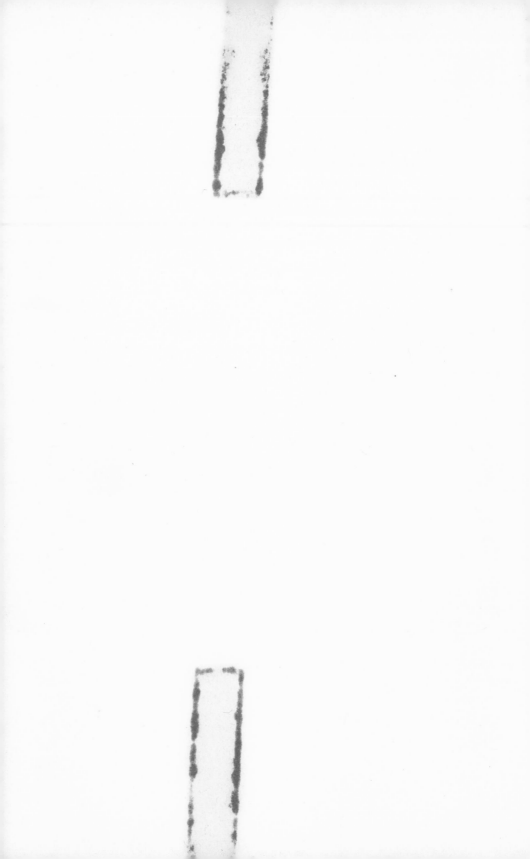

The Political Philosophy
of Spinoza

The Political Philosophy
of Spinoza

By ROBERT J. McSHEA

 Columbia University Press
NEW YORK & LONDON 1968

Preface

*Matters which by their nature are easily perceived cannot be expressed
so obscurely as to be unintelligible.*[1]

THIS is a new book, written about some books by Spinoza
that are now old books. In one of his books, Spinoza explains
that there are two kinds of old books, those that are self-
explanatory, such as the *Elements* of Euclid or some plain
histories, and those, such as the Bible or *Orlando Furioso*, that
are not. The first kind speaks directly to the reader by means
of universally known concepts and logical connections, or by
the narration of events that fall within the range of our
ordinary expectations. The second kind puzzles us; without
more explanation than is contained in the texts themselves, we
cannot tell what they mean.

Spinoza's distinction raises two important questions: Which
of his alternative categories contains his own books? What is
the meaning of the distinction itself?

It is certain that Spinoza intended his own books to be of the
sort written by Euclid or Thucydides, books which need no
commentary and which continue through the centuries to
reach intelligent readers equally well in any language. This
intention has been only partially realized. When his friends, in
the very year of his death, published his works, they prefaced
the selections from his correspondence as follows: "The Let-

[1] TTP (Dover), VII, 112–13.

ters of Certain Learned Men to B. d. S. and the Author's
Replies, Contributing not a Little to the Elucidation of his
Other Works." The erosion of immediate intelligibility has
continued since then, least seriously in the case of his metaphysical and ethical doctrines, most seriously where he applies
those doctrines to political philosophy.

The second question is about the meaning of Spinoza's
distinction. It should be noted that it is books, not subject
matters, which are divided into the categories of the obscure
and the lucid. Authors may be confused, dishonest, or ignorant, and their messages may become garbled in transmission,
but the structure and proceedings of Nature, which is the
topic of all discourse, are always coherent. It is possible to
write books that are permanently intelligible because reality,
both totally and in detail, is also intelligible and constant.

As Spinoza's discussion of books presupposes his ontology
and epistemology, so also it serves as an introduction to his
political thought. His analysis of old books is preliminary to a
critique of the most famous of old books, the Bible. From
there we are led to the subject of religion itself, to its place in
society, and to the nature of society and the state. Because it is
so important to our understanding of Spinoza's political ideas
that we see them as a part of his whole thought, as part of an
intellectual sequence, I have followed the method of explicat-
ing his system rather than his texts.

Spinoza attempted to construct a philosophical orrery, a
conceptual model of reality which would include, relate, and
explain all of existence. It is not necessary to enter into a
discussion of the validity of such an attempt. What he actually
did was to talk at three levels of generality in a single set of
terms.

The most general level of discourse is about the character of
the universe. Of the general principles established, those
which will most concern us are the unity of all things, the
positive effort of each individual thing to preserve itself, and

the denial to Nature of free will, morality, or final causation. The second level is concerned with individual men whose nature and circumstances are understood in terms derived from the more general model. Here we learn of the problems and meaning of human survival and see objective value, denied to things in general, come into existence as a function of the human struggle. The third level is about the interaction of men in society, and here the discourse is of the necessities and possibilities of social existence, the place of sustaining myth and of reason, and the lessons of experience.

Spinoza does not himself confuse these three topics, nor forget the character of their relationships, but he sometimes interweaves and combines them in ways that puzzle the unwary reader. When, for instance, he says that pity and remorse are weaknesses, that promises are to be kept only at convenience, that natural right equals natural power, he is to be related, not to the Thrasymachus of Plato's *Republic*, but rather to that prisoner in the myth of the cave, who returns to the shadow world from the sight of the sun and is accounted mad or blasphemous by those whose only reality is the interplay of shadows.

As for the general purpose of this book, I see it not as a substitute for the reading of Spinoza, nor as the occasion for the introduction of novelties in the interpretation of his thought, nor yet as an explication of various knotty problems to be found in his writings, but simply as an attempt to clarify some of his central ideas on man, society, and government.

ROBERT J. McSHEA

June, 1967

Acknowledgments

❖

I WISH to acknowledge the help given me by Herbert A. Deane and Julian Franklin, who read several preliminary versions of this work, and by Robert D. Cumming and Orest Ranum, who discussed many particular points with me. The several contributions of my wife, Naomi, and my children, Sarah and Daniel, are more complex and less definable. At a family conference after dinner we decided to assume collective responsibility for all errors of fact or inadequacies of understanding.

Contents

❖

CITATION OF SPINOZA'S WORKS

The principal text used is: *Benedict de Spinoza: The Political Works*, edited and translated by A. G. Wernham (Oxford: Clarendon Press, 1958). All references to the *Tractatus Theologico-Politicus* and to the *Tractatus Politicus* are to this edition, except that where the Wernham edition omits a passage, reference is to the Dover edition of Elwes's translation, Volume I of *The Chief Works of Benedict de Spinoza* (New York: Dover Publications, 1951), for example, "TTP (Dover), VII, 98."

The following abbreviations are used in the footnotes:

TTP   *Tractatus Theologico-Politicus*
TP   *Tractatus Politicus*
E   *Ethics* (all page references are to Volume II of the Dover edition of Spinoza)
TdIE *Tractatus de Intellectus Emendatione* (page references to the same volume as that containing the *Ethics*)

Other works by Spinoza, and his correspondence, are cited in full.

I

Life and Writings of Spinoza

*The figure of Benedictus de Spinoza appeared to his contemporaries,
as it has often since appeared to readers, remote and even obscure.
Of all the great seventeenth-century philosophers, Spinoza's life
and the sources of his thought are least known.*[1]

SPINOZA was born in 1632 into the Jewish community which
had recently established itself in Amsterdam. The members
of that community were Sephardics, heirs of the Jewish cultural renaissance that had taken place, a few hundred years before, within the Islamic civilization in Spain. The Moslems
had been intermittent persecutors; with their final victory at
the end of the fifteenth century, the Spanish Christians em-
barked on a campaign to eliminate all non-Christians from
Spain. In the half century following Ferdinand, the national
policy in regard to Jews—convert, emigrate, or die—had been
accomplished, and only the converts remained. Even these
New Christians, "Marranos," were often hounded by popular
prejudice. In the sixteenth century many went to Portugal and,
finding matters no better there, to the only place remaining in
Europe where an urbane Jewish community could exist—
Amsterdam. The founding contingent arrived there in 1593,
about the time when it appeared likely that the Dutch would
succeed in their struggle for independence from Spain. The
principle of religious toleration was but tenuously established
in the Netherlands at this time and did not extend to Jews,

[1] Colie, "Spinoza and the Early English Deists," XX, 23.

but the practice was supported by custom and by the general understanding of the necessities of war and commerce.[2]

In the course of several generations of outward conformity to Catholic doctrine and ritual, the members of the newly founded Jewish community had lost much of their own tradition; they had continued to be Jewish more, perhaps, because they were called so than for any other reason.[3] In their new circumstances, almost as converts to their own religion, they tended more toward enthusiasm for doctrinal and ritual purity than is usual with more settled groups. Although one of the prime requirements for the survival of the group was that it preserve its inner unity and not attract attention, by the time Spinoza had reached maturity, it already had a complex history of intense inner conflict on religious questions.

Spinoza lived completely within this little society [4] until he was twenty, and partly within it until he was excommunicated in 1656, when he was almost twenty-four. Spanish was his native tongue; [5] he learned Hebrew in the community school; he acquired enough Dutch to speak easily with his gentile friends but never became proficient in writing it.[6] In his early twenties he learned Latin, "the language of the priests"; his doing so was a major step out of his own tradition into that of European thought as a whole.

Attempts to establish a specifically Jewish element in Spinoza's mature thought have not produced strikingly successful results. No doubt his religious training directed his interest toward and equipped him to handle those problems of Jewish scholasticism which he attempted to solve, in altered form, in his metaphysics.[7] That training and the cultural milieu of his youth must have been profoundly determinative of the secret

---

[2] Schöffer, p. 68; Barker, p. 124.
[3] Vlekke, p. 186.
[4] Boxer, p. 129, puts the Jewish population in Amsterdam at 1200 in 1655.
[5] Wolf, *Correspondence*, p. 407.
[6] *Ibid.*, Ep. 19, p. 151; Richter, p. 11.
[7] McKeon, pp. 40–43.

springs of his character and outlook, yet all of Spinoza's important ideas are a part of, or a development of, the general European philosophic tradition.

After his excommunication, Spinoza had no further dealings with the Jewish community. For a time he lived in a community of Collegiants, a sect of Mennonites or "Anabaptists," and seems to have been favorably inclined toward, and possibly even very generally influenced by them. However, he never joined any religious sect or even assimilated himself to the secular Dutch community.[8]

We know little of the manner of Spinoza's induction into the world of science and philosophy beyond the fact that it most probably started when he went to study Latin at the school of Van den Ende, a talented political and religious radical.[9] For the twenty-one years between his excommunication in 1656 and his death in 1677, Spinoza lived in but not of the Christian community, composing his philosophy and earning a meager living polishing lenses. He was not isolated. He corresponded with and met the most distinguished scientists and philosophers of that day and had sympathizers and friends among the educated and politically powerful of the Netherlands. But although he was not isolated, he was yet alone, and in more than one sense. He lived alone; his friends were intellectual friends; he was not active in any social or political community. Of his character, as exemplified by his manner of living and style of discourse, it is perhaps sufficient to say that it was in accord with the ethical ideal of his own philosophy.[10]

Problems in the Texts

All of Spinoza's major works were written in Latin. His Latin was adequate but the manuscripts contain some gram-

[8] Note the phrase "We Hebrews," at TTP (Dover), I, 20.
[9] Colerus, p. 3: "He taught his Scholars something else besides Latin. For it was discovered at last, that he sowed the first Seeds of Atheism in the Minds of those Young Boys."
[10] Lucas, pp. 59, 64.

matical errors and he made few attempts at elegance of expression. It has been said that the vernaculars of the time were more suited to the expression of new thought, that the use of Latin condemned a writer to the thrashing of straw, to the fruitless rearrangement of concepts that had with time lost all concrete reference. Spinoza had no choice; his other languages were even less suited than was Latin to his subject or to his prospective readers. Further, he did not write as one introducing novelties or as rejecting what had gone before. It was his intellectual habit of mind to work within the philosophical traditions he had inherited or which were currently accepted in his time, and, almost subversively, to transform them completely but yet according to their own rules.[11] Latin had two advantages for his purposes: it was entirely formal and abstract; as a dead language it lacked the poetic ambiguity and rhetoric of the senses available to languages tied to daily life. It was largely inaccessible to just that element, the more fanatical Calvinists, which in his environment was potentially most dangerous to him.

Concealment

There are various degrees of, methods for, and incentives to the concealment of one's complete thought in writing. An understanding of Spinoza's practice in this matter is important but, fortunately, not difficult. We may mention two considerations which ruled his expression.

First, the safety of society. Because the majority of men are ruled by opinion rather than by force or reason, and because the maintenance of society is a duty for all men of understanding, it is important that a philosopher not contribute to the dissolution of social myths and thereby risk a return either to anarchy or despotism. Of course most men do not read at all, and fewer still can or will read serious books in Latin. Of

[11] Roth, *Spinoza, Descartes and Maimonides*, p. 56; Wolfson, I, 80, 89.

those who do, some can be raised to the level of rational thought and most of the rest can be placated by a sprinkling throughout the text of pious, if irrelevant, concurrences with the prevailing orthodoxy. Spinoza had reason to be more daring, however, than those of his fellow-thinkers who were governed by the same consideration for the stability of society. With the advent of the new science men were about to enter into a new and better era; the possibility of improving the condition of mankind justified taking some risks with social stability.[12]

Second, the danger of persecution. We must look to considerations of personal safety, his own and that of his friends, as the principal motive for Spinoza's tactfulness. Here too, he had more liberty than did most of his contemporaries. His own personal ambition presented no problem—he had none. His only hostages to fortune were his life and his desire to complete his philosophical writing. As for friends, he headed no identifiable school which could be persecuted in his name.[13] Further, the Netherlands was more committed both in principle and in practice to the toleration of unorthodox ideas than was any other European nation.[14] Books that could not be printed elsewhere were printed there;[15] what instruments of censorship existed were disorganized and applied only intermittently. Finally, Spinoza could count on the influence in his behalf of a small but powerful part of the ruling class. They were not, in general, Spinozists, but he and they agreed on so many practical political matters that some writers have found it possible to assert that Spinoza was the political ideologist of the group supporting Jan DeWitt, the *de facto* ruler of the Netherlands from 1653 to 1672.

[12] TTP (Dover), XIV, 189.
[13] Wolf, *Correspondence*, p. 479, notes that the names of his correspondents were omitted in the first edition of Spinoza's letters (1677).
[14] Wolf, *Correspondence*, Ep. 7, p. 100.
[15] *Ibid.*, Ep. 68, p. 334; Ep. 70, p. 339.

The steps which Spinoza took to protect himself against attack are fairly transparent: the use of the appeasive term "God" in place of "Nature" or "Substance"; the elaborate respect paid to the person of Christ; [16] the failure to draw explicitly those conclusions against the truth of religion which yet follow very clearly from his metaphysics; the combination of a dry, deductive method of argument with the employment of words in very precise and very unusual senses. [17] Finally, of those works which express his own opinion, only the *Tractatus Theologico-Politicus* was published in his own lifetime, and that anonymously. The scandal created by this work shows the thinness of the concealment employed in it; the fact that Spinoza published no more during his lifetime is related to this scandal and to the fact that his authorship soon became known. [18]

Contemporary necessities for concealment are perhaps less urgent than in Spinoza's day, certainly they are different. From our own experience we know, however, that when a system of concealing meaning is employed in writing, a counter-system for reading between the lines will evolve. For purposes of our own understanding of Spinoza's writings we will do well to take seriously the belief of his contemporaries that he was the most subversive of philosophers. No doubt they very commonly missed the full thrust of his argument, [19] but they were accurately and keenly aware that it was their ox which was gored.

There are further difficulties in understanding Spinoza which were not intended by him. For example, the language of philosophy has changed since the seventeenth century. Some terms have evolved into opposite meanings, others have

[16] TTP (Dover) I, 18–19; X, 156.

[17] TTP, V, 101.

[18] It was known very soon and very widely. Pufendorf's "refutation," published in 1672, names Spinoza as the author of the *Tractatus Theo-logico-Politicus*.

[19] Colie, *Light and Enlightenment*, p. 114.

become overlaid with additional meaning.[20] Also, Spinoza's style of writing is very condensed. His frugality with illustrations of his meaning, and his tendency to use the same illustrations again and again is sometimes frustrating to the student seeking a full grasp of his thought. Of the major philosophers, he is among the least willing to illuminate a bare conceptual outline with that revelation of personality which often allows us to guess at a meaning which is not completely expressed. But the principal difficulty, for most of us, arises out of the disgraceful shortness of our span of attention, a lack of practice in precise thought following from definitions, and the human tendency to reduce all thought to the level of slogan or cliché.

Too much should not be made of these problems. A grasp of the central message of the *Ethics*, Spinoza's most difficult major work, can be had on a first reading and without any previous study of philosophy, by any sufficiently motivated student.

History of the Texts

Spinoza published only one work under his own name, an uncritical exposition, in "geometric form," of the philosophy of Descartes. The *Tractatus Theologico-Politicus* was published anonymously in 1670. The *Ethics*, the *Tractatus de Intellectus Emendatione*, and the *Tractatus Politicus* were all published in 1677, after his death in that year, but the first two were completed long before then. Except for the apparent fact that the *Tractatus Politicus*, written after the murder of DeWitt in 1672, reflects a more sober or pessimistic political outlook, the dates of composition are of interest only to the specialist. Spinoza's writings show no significant change of outlook in time.

The subsequent history of these writings is curious. The

[20] Hubbeling, pp. 23, 46; E, II, def. 6; Wolf, *Correspondence*, Ep. 12, p. 116.

initial fame, or notoriety, of Spinoza up to the last decade of the eighteenth century was based entirely on the *Tractatus Theologico-Politicus*.[21] This work had a wide circulation and great influence on the Enlightenment.[22] Published references to it are rare except in the form of refutations and invective.[23] It was an underground book, published under the imprint of publishers who did not exist; it appeared on bookshelves as a cookbook, as a prayerbook, as any kind of book which would not attract attention. Spinoza was bracketed with Hobbes as an "atheist," clearly as the worse of the pair. Although Spinoza had many secret sympathizers, no one of note cared to be identified publicly with his doctrines.[24] Locke, for example, knew the doctrines of Hobbes and of the Spinoza of the *Tractatus Theologico-Politicus* quite well, but mentioned their evil reputations as well-deserved and described his own knowledge of them as slight.[25] Although he had had a number of conversations with Spinoza, Leibnitz always minimized or denied this acquaintance. Hume spoke of Spinoza's naturalistic metaphysics as "the hideous hypothesis" of "that famous atheist,"[26] the better perhaps to conceal the extent of his own adherence to it.[27] But even Kant did not read the *Ethics*; its

[21] Roth, *Spinoza*, p. 177; Collingwood, p. 179; Colie, *Spinoza and the Early English Deists*, p. 32.

[22] Hazard, pp. 139, 144–50; Stephen, I, 33: "The whole essence of the deist position may be found in Spinoza's *Tractatus Theologico-Politicus*."

[23] Elwes, I, vi–vii; Dunner, p. 1; Cassirer, p. 187; Eckstein, pp. 268–69.

[24] Duff, p. 8.

[25] *The Works of John Locke*, IV, 477: "I am not so well read in Hobbes or Spinoza as to be able to say what were their opinions in this matter. But possibly there be those who will think your lordship's authority of more use to them in the case than those justly decried names . . ."

[26] Hume, *A Treatise of Human Nature*, p. 241.

[27] Duff, p. 8: "The resemblances, for example, between his [Spinoza's] views and those of Hume, and not less on Politics than on Ethics, seem to be too pronounced and specific to be explicable otherwise than by supposing Hume to have had a direct knowledge of his predecessor's work. The melodramatic references to the 'hideous hypothesis' and the 'atheistic philosophy' are in the fashion of the day, and rather confirm than refute this supposition"; Pollock, *Spinoza: His Life and Philosophy*, p. 356: "It appears, however, that Berkeley had really read Spinoza; which is more than can be said of either Locke or Hume."

fame dates from the period immediately after him and its impact on German idealism is well known.[28] From that period onward it becomes impossible to trace Spinoza's influence: Nietzsche acknowledges it,[29] Whitehead does not, and in neither case can we judge its real extent. During the first half of the nineteenth century, self-styled Spinozists were common in England, particularly in literary circles. Coleridge, Shelley, George Eliot, Byron, and Wordsworth [30] were among them. The German Romantics honored Spinoza as a forerunner of their own outlooks; it is still a question whether we most truly see his philosophy as an early and crude version of that of Hegel, or Hegelianism as one of many possible variations on a theme by Spinoza.[31] In general, the moralizing nineteenth century venerated Spinoza as the ultimate in disinterested morality, missing or ignoring the real bite of his uncompromising naturalism and determinism. The aura of sentimentality about his name and the persistent attempt to reduce his teachings to the capacities of middle-class cultural aspiration date from that era.

Spinoza has been hailed as the father of psychoanalysis because of his insistence on psychic determinism,[32] his view of the passions as natural phenomena,[33] his deduction of the passions from the primitive element of self-preservation,[34] his insistence on the unity of mind and body,[35] and his belief that the power of the unenlightened passions can be dissipated in the process of understanding them.[36] It seems true that the

[28] Hubbeling, p. 1; Elwes, p. viii; Cassirer, *Philosophy of the Enlightenment*, p. 190; Eckstein, pp. 269–79, argues that Rousseau had read the *Ethics*.

[29] Kaufman, p. 116: "I have a precursor, and what a precursor!"

[30] Metzger, pp. 279–93; Grabo, pp. 43–50; Elwes, p. ix.

[31] Roth, *Spinoza*, p. 217; Wolstein, p. 441.

[32] TdIE, p. 32; E, V, prop. 40; Bidney, p. 375; Kohut, p. 480; Waelder, "Psychic Determinism and the Possibility of Prediction," p. 15; Brenner, p. 3.

[33] E, IV, n. 57.

[34] Meerloo, p. 893.

[35] Wolf, *Correspondence*, Eps. 17, p. 140 and 68A, p. 331; Hubbeling, pp. 43, 77.

[36] E, V, props. 3, 4; E, V, prop. 15; E, V, n. 20.

systematic, theoretical "anticipation" by Spinoza of some of the elements of psychoanalytic theory is more noteworthy than the striking but random insights of literary artists such as Schopenhauer and Nietzsche. It is not at all clear, however, what is accomplished in stressing this connection. Certainly Spinoza is in no direct way the founder of modern psychology.

As for the influence of Spinoza's specifically political thought—it is almost as though he had not written. Until late in the nineteenth century, no well-known writer other than Pufendorf [37] notices him as a political philosopher.[38] We know that Hume, Locke, and Rousseau were acquainted with Spinoza's political writings, and we have no difficulty in finding many anticipations of their thought in his works; to proceed from this point to the assertion of an influence is a difficult and perhaps impossible task.

Even today, Spinoza's political philosophy is slighted, and sometimes misrepresented, in standard works on the subject. The reasons for this neglect are several: aside from the fact that he "spilled the beans" prematurely on the matter of the existence of God and the truth of the revealed religions, and even of deism,[39] his political thought is too radically enlightened, particularly in his rejection of natural law and of the theory of the rights of man, to be of use for the relatively limited aims of the Enlightenment; he was too abstract for the Utilitarians, too naturalistic for the Romantics, too metaphysical and dogmatic (or shall we say too philosophically engaged?) for the moderns. His political philosophy, meant to fit all ages, has been accepted, has been taken seriously, by none. Even that ruling class in the Netherlands to which his theory was in the first place addressed was permanently out of power five years before his death.

[37] Pufendorf, II, 159.
[38] Vaughan, *The Political Writings of Jean-Jacques Rousseau*, II, 9.
[39] Randall, I, 702.

If this is the verdict of history, then it must be reversed. The following study of Spinoza's political philosophy is primarily explicative in intent, yet it is hoped that it will also contribute toward the recovery of that philosophy as a body of thought which is yet alive and relevant to our concerns.

II

Background

◆

. . . we should know what was the occasion, the time, the age, in which each book was written, and to what nation it was addressed.[1]

PERHAPS nowhere is the principle of multiple determination better illustrated than in the writings of a major political philosopher, and nowhere is the fallacy of reductionism better shown than in the attempt to see him as reacting solely to the local political situation or solely to the permanent metaphysical problems—to cite the extreme cases. To some extent, what we mean by the term "major thinker" is someone who integrates the widest spectrum of experience into the simplest and most adequate formulations.

The reasons for not treating Spinoza's works as completely lucid in themselves have already been mentioned. It remains to remark that in giving a background to his thought, we are not committing ourselves either to historicism or to the pure intellectualism implied in the phrase "permanent problems." Nor would Spinoza himself have done so: he held that each man is thoroughly determined by his environment, history, and heredity to do and think what he does, and to be what he is, but that environment, history, and heredity are parts of an integrated world order within which men may discover themselves as meaningful, and in a sense even valuable, creatures.

[1] TTP (Dover), VII, 103.

Much of the relevance and spirit of Spinoza's writings is lost if we do not have some idea of the whole situation as it presented itself to him. The purpose of this chapter is to suggest, in elementary fashion, some of the leading elements of that situation of which we have some knowledge.

Philosophical Background

Spinoza's metaphysics employs the terminology and treats of the problems of two strains of thought—Jewish scholasticism and Cartesianism. In noting this first instance of his habit of working within traditional lines as far as possible, we must realize that his thought is in no useful sense a blend or reconciliation of its two components; he used the materials at hand, with a minimum of concern for what objects they may originally have served. Jewish scholasticism was the content of his early training; Cartesianism was the then almost universally accepted outlook of intellectuals. Spinoza first came to public notice as an expert expositor of the philosophy of Descartes.

It is generally understood that Jewish scholasticism was the equivalent in some major respects of Arabic and Christian scholasticisms. The problem for each, throughout its development, was the same: the reconciliation of faith and reason; the reconciliation, that is, of a religious text partly written and wholly understood in the light of that magical vision of the world which became routinized as neo-Platonism, with the rational pronouncements of a Greek philosopher, Aristotle. No allowance could be made for possible corruption of the authoritative text or for the historical circumstances of its composition; the neo-Platonic accretion was not only the work of ancient canonized authorities with a standing equal to that of the text, it was also the very world view of the scholastics themselves. The text of Aristotle was partial, corrupt, and incompletely understood—we can now only dimly perceive the power of his appeal to the best medieval minds. The motive for their improbable undertaking was indistinguishably both philosophical and theological. The problems discussed which relate to our present study were:

How to reconcile the goodness of God with the existence of evil? Answers were found in the necessary consequence of man's free will, in the incorrigibility of matter, in the imperfections gradually coming into existence in the long, possibly infinite, descending chain of spirits connecting God with the world,[2] in evil as illusion, in evil as a kind of sluggishness in those things of a nature most different from that of God.

How can man's free will be reconciled with God's foreknowledge? By obscuring the difference between that foreknowledge which God must have and that which men may sometimes have, some found it possible to say that knowledge of a future event left that event yet contingent; some denied free will; some thought that God might not allow himself to foresee some things; many abandoned the question to the realm of mystery.

Does God will a Good which is good independently of his will, or is the Good defined simply as his will? [3] In the former case, God is subject to a standard which is beyond his power to affect, which is by definition impossible. In the latter case there are two possibilities, each of which raises a problem: either the Good can be known only through direct knowledge of the will of God (revelation) and through its most recent revelation (because God has free will and can change his arbitrary definition of Good), *or* God's determination of value is expressed in nature, as natural law, and can be discovered by natural means. The first alternative leads to religious anarchy; by the second, God has bound himself so completely by his original determination as to lose his freedom and become no more than the laws of nature, while the Scriptures become supererogatory.

Similarly, what is God's relation to Reason? If the validity

[2] Lovejoy, p. 59.
[3] E, I, prop. 33, n. 2.

of the reasoning process is not dependent on God's will, then he is subject to it, which is "absurd." On the other hand, if the rational process is the arbitrary will of God, then it is changeable and therefore unknowable, or it is unchangeable, knowable, and can be used to criticize revelation and authority.

What is God's relation to the universe? If God is a Spirit, and the universe is all or partly material, in what way can one affect the other unless they are also limited by each other? [4] Is God's relation to things transcendent or immanent?

Because to define is to limit, and to limit is to negate, does not any positive statement about God limit him and therefore do that which is impossible? If God is perfect, complete, how can he be affected by joy or sorrow on account of man,[5] or even be aware of his existence? How, in fact, can God do anything at all, without thereby implying a previous condition of unrealized purpose, of imperfection? If God is completely free, is he not then the very principle of anarchy, unbound not only by his promises and goodness but even by his prescience? Do not, in fact, the very perfections ascribed to God combine to reduce his freedom to nothing and make of him an empty principle?

Finally, at a lower level of abstraction, was the problem which Plato found in dealing with the Homeric works: *How to reconcile the Biblical account of God as visible, revengeful, forgetful, remorseful, with any coherent idea of God at all?* [6]

These questions are neither a complete nor a representative compilation of the questions treated of by the scholastics; they do represent some of the main lines of Spinoza's interest in those problems as he encountered them in the Jewish commentators. Some writers have found it useful to consider Spinoza as the last of the scholastics, so prominent in his philosophy does his preoccupation with some of their problems ap-

[4] Wolfson, I, 91.
[5] E, V, prop. 17.
[6] Wolf, *Correspondence*, Ep. 36, pp. 223–24.

pear.[7] We might well question this approach, for although Spinoza does offer solutions to problems of the sort mentioned above, he does so only after radically transforming the meaning of the questions themselves. Unlike Descartes, who evidently meant to ignore the old structure of thought and to build anew, Spinoza went back to it to blow it up, or rather to dismantle it, and to use the pieces for a new construction.

The medieval scholastic enterprise endured for the better part of a millenium, infinitely various in its manifestations yet always identifiable as an approach, and died, with the view of reality which it expressed, a lingering death.[8] Descartes was but one of its gravediggers, but historians of philosophy have chosen him as the most effective of them all. No doubt no single part of his method was quite original, yet the complete method, with its criterion of truth, dependence on reason, rejection of the principle of authority in most matters, assumption of the mathematically describable nature of the motions in nature, and its metaphysical anchorage in the certainties of intuitions which could claim both public and private acceptance was, for the seventeenth century, the accepted weapon for the intellectual battle against the feudal outlook. It is perhaps a measure of his originality that he raised more questions than he solved.

Briefly and perhaps tendentiously, let us recall that Descartes, starting from the demonstration of the existence of the doubting mind, had gone on to establish the independent status of the world of thought. Using a version of the ontological proof, he confirmed the existence of God and of some of his attributes. Finally, from the truthfulness of God, he deduced the reality of the extended world and the inner coherence and external relevance of reason. Carried over from the older

---

[7] Wolfson, I, vii, 80; McKeon, pp. 29, 49–51.

[8] It is a moot question whether the death of scholasticism is represented by the final victory of Aristotle over Plotinus or by the sudden decay of the authority of Aristotle himself. Neither movement was quite completed in the period we are discussing.

viewpoint was a belief in the transcendence of God, in man's free will, and in miracles and the authority of Scripture.

Spinoza had no quarrel with some of Descartes's objectives: the establishment of reason, or working from clear and certain notions as the ultimate or first authority for belief; clearing a place for science in a natural world of determined events; the validation of the relevance of mathematical thought to the uniformities of nature. His objection was that Descartes had not done enough and had not done it well.

The initial and worst error had been in starting from subjectivity. Descartes never really escaped the solipsism implicit in his chosen starting point. Further, granted the establishment of two independent worlds of thought and extension, it proves impossible to explain their relation;[9] one of them must eventually be denied full reality, or be subordinated to the other. Yet materialism cannot account for thought, order, mathematics; idealism cannot account for the world of appearances or even for intersubjective communication.

A major consequence of the radical dichotomization of reality into thought and extension is the failure to establish a rational basis for the ordering of experience, that is to say, science. But even before he reaches this point, Descartes has involved himself in a dilemma: the validity of reason must be assumed in order to prove the existence of the world of thought and of God, yet God himself is later taken to be the guarantor of the validity of the process by which his existence is demonstrated. The further problem of the relation of God to reason is as perplexing in the philosophy of Descartes as it was for the scholastics.[10]

Finally, in allowing free will—indeterminacy—to God and the mind of man, Descartes opened the window to all the irrationalism and gothic miracle-mongering which he had just thrown out the door. Descartes wrote in a society in which

[9] Descartes, *Philosophical Works of Descartes*, I, 172, 216.
[10] Roth, *Spinoza, Descartes and Maimonides*, pp. 34, 36.

humanist scepticism was common in higher circles; the full-blown metaphysical scepticism of the Enlightenment is partly traceable to this incoherence.[11]

It has been said that Spinoza's metaphysics is an attempted solution of explicit problems raised by Jewish scholasticism and by Descartes; a solution, moreover, attempted in the very terms in which the problems are raised. It should not be thought that this base was too narrow for a comprehensive philosophy. Jewish scholasticism is fairly representative of medieval philosophy, and that in turn contains within it most of the central problems and lines of solution contained in ancient philosophy.[12] Cartesianism, on its part, for all its apparent contradictions and ambiguities, was the first clear statement of an approach to metaphysics that has been influential up to the present time.

Science and Scientific Thought

The idea of science—as a body of verifiable empirical generalizations, as an ongoing activity of cooperative research into all natural causes with consensual standards of relevance, truth, and interest, as the institutionalization of a technique that was expected to produce significant changes in man's life and beliefs—was born before Spinoza, but came to maturity in his lifetime. That lifetime was overlapped by that of Galileo, who formulated the basic concepts of physics, and that of Newton, who brought the heavens and the earth under one iron law of matter in motion.

"Science," as an institution, is a seventeenth-century creation. Formal academies and a literature came into being; specialization began; ingenious apparatus and techniques were developed for counting, measuring, seeing, and discriminating those elements of experience to be studied; basic concepts were formulated; a scientific community, complete with theo-

[11] Ibid., pp. 10, 38; TTP, IV, 71.
[12] McKeon, pp. 40, 50.

rists, experimenters, popularizers, purists, charlatans, and a nonparticipating but fascinated lay public came into existence.

The conflict of science with religion was at once apparent because some of the earliest theories happened to conflict not only with popular opinion and with that of the followers of the Philosopher, but also with the explicit word of God as expressed in the Bible. Even if the earliest discoveries had been made in less sensitive areas, it must have been evident to all that scientists were engaged in a kind of activity which had no relevance either to salvation or to sin. Sinners of all kinds, witches, usurers, and human devils, were familiar types known for indifference to eternal punishment, but their existence rather exemplified, than implied a general scepticism of, the current world view.

Yet the activities of scientists could not be completely condemned; their empiricism, and their methods of rational analysis as applied to natural phenomena, were too similar to like attitudes and techniques then coming into use in commerce, war, and government. Acts of God were now insurable; the cold calculation of probabilities brought wealth, power, and success in war and elsewhere more certainly than did prayer or adherence to the old wisdom. The success of science, not only in the production of practical gadgetry but in its arousal and satisfaction of curiosity and in its ability to inspire confidence by its reasonableness and by the public character of its demonstrations,[13] raised the conflict of science with religion to the level of a confrontation of two world views. What view of reality did the success of science imply and, conversely, what view of reality implied the validity of the scientific effort?

The questions raised by this confrontation could be stated in the same terms employed by medieval thinkers,[14] although with the usual result that follows the putting of new wine into

[13] TTP (Dover), I, 14.
[14] McKeon, p. 28.

old bottles. Aristotle versus Harvey, Scripture versus Coperni-
cus, are variations of the authority-faith versus reason theme.
The assumption of the uniformity of nature is intimately
related to the concept of the unchanging character of God's
will and of his absolute control over nature, or to the idea that
nature is the living exemplification of God's reason. The problem of the relation of spirit to matter is a form of the
thought-extension dichotomy and so is connected, on the one
hand, to the epistemological paradoxes raised by the distinction between primary and secondary qualities, and on the
other hand to the ontological question of the relation of mathematics to motion, of scientific generality to its concrete exemplification.[15] The religious idea of the unity of God, and of
all things in God, that is, the belief that God is the only fully
existing being, is transformed (most clearly by Spinoza) into
the scientific assumption of a single order of nature.

At a more prosaic level, the progress of science appeared to
demand: (1) A theory of the uniformity of nature and of
nature as one and all-inclusive (this meant the rejection of
dualism, epistemological or ontological, and the acceptance of
determinism, psychic as well as physical);[16] (2) The rejection
of teleology as a principle of explanation and reliance only on
the principle of efficient causation; (3) A theory of knowledge and a criterion of truth.

Practical Politics
Spinoza's political writings are only marginally a commentary
on contemporary European politics, so far as his explicit statements go, but he was well informed, not only of events but of
their meaning.

The seventeenth century witnessed the demonstration of
the advantages of centralized monarchic power and secular-

---

[15] "Exemplification": The imprecision is deliberate; there seems no point
in taking a stand here on currently controverted matters of terminology in
the philosophy of science.
[16] E, II, prop. 7; E, I, prop. 33, n. 2.

ized politics. The anarchic German states floundered misera-
bly through the Thirty Years' War; Spain steadily declined,
locked in religious intolerance; England's civil wars greatly
reduced her possible role in European affairs; only France,
willing on occasion to treat with heretic and infidel and well
under the control of its king or his minister, was in a position
to consider the possibility of dominating Europe. France was
the model of the new secular state; its endless and widely
discussed maneuvers for advantage, relatively unhindered by
internal conflict, were a standing lesson in political realities
and possibilities. Two republican regimes which flourished in
the middle of the century, in England and in the Netherlands,
both came to an end in Spinoza's lifetime; his writings indicate
the major influence on his thought exerted by these events.

The Dutch Situation

Some reference to the history and peculiar political institutions of the Dutch Republic seems necessary.[17] The Netherlands was a federation of seven provinces, of which Holland,
containing the city of Amsterdam, was the principal. Holland
accounted for more than half the wealth and population of the
Netherlands and contributed more than half the taxes.

Throughout the first half of the seventeenth century, the
Netherlands was, by almost any criterion, the most advanced
nation in Europe. The population was about two-thirds that
of England; the amount of Dutch shipping equaled that of all
the rest of Europe combined;[18] the general standard of living
there was unequaled elsewhere.[19] The Netherlands was a trading state; it produced much less food than it consumed; its
watery land was almost destitute of raw materials. Although it
had a highly profitable colonial empire in the Far East, the real
bases of its wealth were the cheap and efficient shipment and

[17] Clark, p. 13.
[18] Temple, I, 182.
[19] Barker, p. 204; Boxer, p. 54, however, notes another side of the picture.

the success and of the failure of the Dutch Republic. It is clearly not the sort of constitution by which Kant proposed to rule a race of devils, but one which presupposes considerable political maturity, a capacity for compromise, and a strong sense of common purpose or interest. It was government by persuasion, but persuasion directed toward concrete interests rather than toward principle. The influence of this system on Spinoza's political thought will become evident.

During the height of Dutch power, up to 1672, the Netherlands were ruled by an elite of about 2,000 members, an untitled aristocracy[30] of "old money," selected by co-optation.[31] Wealth alone did not gain entry to it, nor did relative slenderness of means invariably exclude.[32] This gentry was well-educated and well-traveled and inclined, in religion, toward a kind of Unitarianism. Although the regent families held much of the stock in major commercial enterprises, particularly in the East India Company,[33] they were not usually active in business.[34] They were the leaders of society and active patrons of the arts and sciences; they ran the nation through their control of the town councils, from which the provincial assemblies and the Estates General were controlled, but they never had the support of the bulk of the population, even in their stronghold, Holland. Their politics has been

[30] Zumthor, pp. 231–32. There *was* a titled aristocracy, but in 1620, only 35 noble families survived in Holland and of these some were impoverished and almost merged with the peasantry. "The nobility lived like exiles in the heart of a nation of traders and merchants."

[31] de la Court, p. 317; Vlekke, p. 162, says 10,000; Barker, pp. 159, 168; Temple, I, 96; Geddes, p. 19, "a close brahminical caste"; Boxer, p. 11; CMH, p. 276, says that in 1672 one man in a thousand, in Holland, belonged to a regent family and, p. 294, that in the same year, there were 500 sitting regents.

[32] Vlekke, p. 163.

[33] Temple, I, 134, 159.

[34] Renier, p. 105, notes that in 1615 most Amsterdam regents were active or retired merchants, whereas by 1652, most were *rentiers;* Geyl, Part II, p. 199; Boxer, pp. 29–31.

described as "Whig," [35] but if they were "Whigs," who was the "king"?

Before the Dutch revolt, the king of Spain ruled the country through a military commander, a stadtholder (Dutch translation of "lieutenant"). By the Union of Utrecht, in 1579, the Dutch abjured allegiance to Philip of Spain on the ground of breach of contract.[36] The then stadtholder, William the Silent, led the revolt and retained the title and the command of the military forces. William's heirs of the House of Orange, however, were stadtholders not of the United Provinces but only of those provinces which happened to elect them to the position. Backed by the power of the name and their own successes in frequent wars, the successive leaders of the House of Orange were identified in the popular mind with the principle of the unity of the country, a principle which then, as later in other nations, had radical populist overtones. The history of the Dutch Republic, therefore, from its founding to the death of DeWitt in 1672, and even after that, is in large part a history of the struggle for control between the ruling oligarchy and the House of Orange. The struggle split the country—behind the stadtholders were ranged a great part of the common people,[37] the Calvinist clergy to a man, the army, most of the petite bourgeoisie, the rural gentry and, from abroad, the English Stuarts.[38] The strength of the oligarchs was concentrated in the province of Holland and depended on their financial control, the navy, the French alli-

[35] Schöffer, p. 66.

[36] Barker, p. 99, says that the Union was not a union but an alliance, and that it was the fundamental law of the Dutch until 1795; the year 1579 was also that of the *Vindiciae contra Tyrannos*.

[37] Temple, I, 117, 160; *CMH*, p. 284; DeWitt estimated, in 1652–53, that one-tenth of one per cent of the people supported the republican regime.

[38] The support by the Stuarts of the House of Orange had two obvious bases: a distaste for republics and the marriage link between the two royal families which later furnished the legitimating factor in the displacement of the Stuarts from the English throne by William of Orange.

ance, the support of religious dissenters, Catholics, and intellectuals, as well as on their class unity and political dexterity.[39] During the century they had two leaders of outstanding ability, the Grand Pensionaries Johan van Oldenbarneveldt and Jan DeWitt.

The office of Grand Pensionary was yet another anomoly of Dutch politics. Each provincial assembly employed a paid official as a secretary. The permanent official, if sufficiently able, commonly became the *de facto* head of the assembly. Because of the preponderance of Holland in the alliance of provinces, the secretary of the assembly of that province was in a good position to dominate the Estates General and the country. Thus from 1653 to 1672, DeWitt, the Grand Pensionary of Holland, was the actual administrator of the affairs of the Netherlands. An act of exclusion, urged upon a willing DeWitt by Cromwell, provided for the abolition of the competing office of stadtholder; the sole male heir of the House of Orange was a minor during all of DeWitt's time in office. The absence of a leader for the Orangists, the political genius of DeWitt, and the fact that during his stewardship the country reached the apogee of its wealth and power, account for the prolongation of the power of the oligarchs in the face of increasing popular hostility. That hostility had a number of grounds: the ruling class was considered lax in religion and morals, weak in regard to the international and domestic menace of Catholicism, it was thought to put class interests ahead of national interests, and its administration was said to be inefficient and corrupt. There was also an ineradicable feeling that middle-class rule was somehow illegitimate.[40]

It should come as no surprise that Spinoza, his friends, and all those who had any claim to be numbered among the men of the Enlightenment, should be supporters of DeWitt.[41]

[39] *CMH*, p. 279; Boxer, pp. 42–43.

[40] Renier, p. 86; Zumthor, p. 234; Boxer, pp. 12–13.

[41] Spinoza's criticisms of monarchy, particularly for the Netherlands, will be noted later. For his criticism of Calvinist mores, see E, IV, 45.

The DeWitt regime stood for religious toleration and for liberality in regard to the expression of opinion; its followers supported the new science of Galileo, the new philosophy of Descartes, and the spirit of the new politics of Hobbes; the Stadtholder-Calvinist coalition threatened a return to dynastic politics, dangerous for a commercial state, and to the repressive uniformity of a chapel dominated society. As we shall see, however, Spinoza was no mere ideologist of the oligarchic cause; he was a severe critic of its failings and an advocate of democracy.

The subsequent decline of the Netherlands has obscured the fact that it produced the first distinctively bourgeois revolution in Europe, a hundred years before the English revolution of 1688 and two hundred years before the French revolution of 1789. This precocity of political development in the land of his adoption makes more plausible the thesis that Spinoza's political ideas were anticipatory of much to come.[42]

Political Thought

The most radical division in Western history since Charlemagne is that between medieval and modern. Whatever the earlier portents, the seventeenth is the century of the actual transition to the most important elements of modernity; however sophisticated (in both senses of the word) it has since become, the basic image of reality formed then is that which we yet hold. Whitehead is not alone in urging us to study the seventeenth century with all the complexity of motives with which we study the original architectural plan of an old house we have acquired. Particularly relevant to our interest is the set of conditions under which our present political concepts were brought into being.

Some of the matters with which political thought had to cope were: the secularization, that is to say, amoralization, of politics in the new nation-state; the final breakdown of the

[42] Renier, p. 23; *CMH*, p. 300.

vision of the unity of Christendom; the end of the view of men as having natural places in a natural society, and the adoption, in every sphere, of the viewpoint of individualism; the subordination of religious to national unity. Of these, reductionist individualism, the assumption that the primary building block of society is the individual man considered apart from his acquired "secondary" qualities—rank, possessions, moral value, social personality—is the most significant. The awful medieval alternative to status in society was slavery or the outlawry of hunted animals, the reduction to the nightmare of subjection to another's naked personal will. Similarly in the philosophical view of man, the end of status, of social teleology, seemed to mean the end of the authority of natural and customary law, and therefore too, of the dignity, value, and even safety, of individual men. It is one of the paradoxes of individualism that when we think away that in a person which seems adventitious or externally imposed, seeking the inner reality, we may find that which we find beneath the layers of an onion—nothing. Political life appeared suddenly to have been reduced to what Augustine described as a banding together of robbers.

This was, and is, the theoretical state of affairs, although some have maintained the validity of traditional views of natural right and natural law to the present day, with barely the minimum ideological figleaf required by decency. Only Hobbes and Spinoza did not quail at the new vision; we shall see later how they fared.

The problem for political theory was: Given the simplified model of the individual as the necessary starting point, and given the absence of a moral directive, such as had been found in natural law or religious authority, and given the passionate and egocentric nature of man, then: What will be the life of men without the state; under what conditions can men come together to live in civil society; what obligation can a man have to obey the commands of the state, or what reasons can

be given to show that it is better for him to do so; what form
must the state take if it is to be able to command the obedience
of its subjects either as a matter of obligation or of interest?
For his answers to these questions, Spinoza drew on two
sources: past political thought and his own metaphysics.

There are a great many political thinkers to whom Spinoza
is, directly or indirectly, demonstrably indebted. Yet, because
not all connections are interesting connections, it is desirable
that a distinction be made between kinds of political thinking.

We may differentiate among: (1) normative politics, as
exemplified in *Mirrors of Princes* and ordinary political exhortation, in which the attempt is made to direct political behavior to conformity with current ideals, without visible concern
with the actual practicability or even ultimate desirability of
such action; (2) value-free political science, which informs us
of actual political facts, describes the structure and dynamics
of given political situations, predicts the probable effects of
alternative actions, and does all this with as much depth as can
be obtained with the aid of the other behavioral sciences and
such stock of private wisdom as the practitioner feels he can
safely expect a heterogeneous public to share; and (3) political theory or political philosophy ("theory," if the metaphysical basis is not made explicit or is inadequate or irrelevant to
the political thought, "philosophy," if the metaphysics is comprehensive and primary and the political thought clearly derives from it), which employs political science in combination
with a theory of human nature and an ethics in order to arrive
at an understanding of man's political life and at a formulation
of suitable goals and of activities appropriate thereto.

For the double reason that the title of this study indicates its
direction toward the third category of political thought, and
that the present chapter is intended to identify the problems
which faced Spinoza rather than to point out every possible
influence, we are excused here from the lengthy task of study-
ing the political ideas of most of his predecessors and contem-

poraries. In fact, with a certain special exception to be made in the case of Machiavelli, and perhaps Calvin, it seems most useful to consider the theoretical background of the political philosophy of Spinoza to consist partly of that of Hobbes and partly of Spinoza's own philosophical system. Although Spinoza wrote much on politics and is clearly in the first rank of political philosophers, he is primarily interested neither in politics nor in metaphysics but in an ethical program for the achievement of personal autonomy. Spinoza intended his political writings to be a practical application of that program; his intent was realized at least to the extent that no adequate study of those writings can avoid continual reference to the antecedent philosophy.

Hobbes qualifies as "background" partly because of his own tremendous force as a political thinker and his temporal proximity, and partly because Spinoza was writing for people many of whom were either Hobbists or quasi-Hobbists.[43] The relation between the two men will be explored in a later chapter.

Spinoza's own philosophy presents for us an enormous problem in the understanding of his political thought. His metaphysics, that part of his writings about which most commentators have busied themselves, are a complex statement of the necessary consequences of necessary assumptions about the nature of the Real. Between the metaphysics and the politics, however, are the ethics, and though Spinoza's explication of his ethical doctrine is conducted with his usual and amazing combination of "geometric method," intransigent naturalism, and hard realism, a grasp of his meaning requires the occurrence of some intuitions which seem not to be universally available. A dialectic may be helpful as a propaedeutic, but the end desired, the direct intuition into reality, cannot be predictably elicited by any method. This final insight produces, or is identical with, salvation: the gaining of oneself as

[43] Wolf, Correspondence, p. 446.

an autonomous being, the losing of oneself as an egoistic creature. This might seem hopelessly to separate politics from ethics, for in relation to salvation, all mundane matters are uninteresting except as they may be helpful to it, or dangerously obstructive.[44] For those who have achieved salvation, the state has little to offer: Plato's philosopher must be forced by society to serve it; for some Stoics and for Augustine the service of the state is an unrewarding and unpleasant duty; for thinkers such as Thoreau, the inner necessity is to disown the world and flee to the woods, or, alternatively, because the world of illusion is also a training ground for the spirit, to defy the state's commands and suffer the consequences of that defiance.

The attempt will be made here to show how, and with what success, Spinoza heals this breach; how, from an ethic of personal salvation, he arrives at a doctrine under which the philosopher engages in political activity not by duty, nor under duress, nor by way of demonstrative gesture, but as a man with concrete realizable goals, goals which offer tangible benefits not only for others but also for himself.[45]

Further, how can Spinoza arrive at a system of ordered political values from an ethic which denies the freedom of choice usually associated with value itself? In a world in which "better" and "worse" are wholly relative to interests, what is the meaning of addressing them to a creature who must do what circumstances, his previous history, and his own nature compel him to do?

[44] TdIE, p. 3; TTP (Dover), II, 39; Augustine *The City of God* xii. 8.
[45] TdIE, pp. 6–7.

III

The Metaphysics

❖

Indeed, it has been the common fate of many readers and critics of Spinoza to stick fast in the First Part of the ETHICS.[1]

SPINOZA's political philosophy is derived from his metaphysics by way of his ethics and cannot be understood without some knowledge of its source. The following brief account of the metaphysics makes no claim to completeness.

The first sentence of the *Ethics* is, "By that which is self-caused, I mean that of which the essence involves existence, or that of which the nature is only conceivable as existent." [2] In the form of a definition, this begins one of the ontological proofs of the existence of God. The ontological proof is certainly the most perplexing of such proofs but, as Spinoza uses it, it is relatively simple. The version which most clearly expresses his method is:

If anything, thought or object, exists, then it exists (a) as the only thing which exists, in which case it is not limited by or related to anything else and so is infinite, complete and eternal (outside of time) and must operate solely out of the laws of its own nature and, for lack of anything outside it must be considered self-caused, or (b) as one of a number of things, each limited by and related to each of the other things, the sum total of all such things constituting, with their inter-

---

[1] Pollock, *Spinoza: His Life and Philosophy,* p. 356.
[2] E, I, def. 1.

relationships, a system which must be regarded in the same light as (a) above.[3]

This totality of things, or principle of the organization of all things, considered in its aspect of unity, independence, and completeness, may be called the Universe; considered as the only existent, it is Reality, or Substance; considered as the complete set of all interactions, it is the Nature [4] in which we live and of which we are a part. Spinoza also called it God.[5]

It should be noticed that the conclusion of the argument is modest. Spinoza believes that he has shown that "all things" constitute a system, he has said nothing about the degree of organization so implied.[6] Further, Spinoza must not be understood in a Kantian sense; the conclusion is ontological, not epistemological; it says, not that we must *experience* all things as an ordered system, but that all things *are* a system.

The system of nature is experienced by men as thought or as extension. These attributes are not reducible the one to the other, yet they are expressions of, or aspects of, the same reality—as a saucer may be called convex or concave, depending upon our view, or as visual and tactile experiences of the same thing are yet not identical experiences. Neither attribute is prior to or more real than the other; the thought is a thought of an object or of a situation; the extended object exemplifies the thought.[7] The attributes are not categories of perception, but unique expressions of the essence of Substance; their number is not limited in any way and thus may be called infinite,[8] though there may not be more than the two mentioned.[9]

The attribute of thought may be likened to a master equa-

---

[3] Saw, pp. 62–73; Hallett, pp. 20, 43; Roth, *Spinoza*, p. 61, and *Spinoza, Descartes and Maimonides*, pp. 51, 57; McKeon, pp. 45, 165–66, 190, 233; Parkinson, pp. 53–54; TTP, IV, 71; E, I, props. 1–17.
[4] TTP, XVI, 127; Wolf, *Correspondence*, Ep. 32, pp. 210–12.
[5] TTP, VI, 89; TTP (Dover), I, 25.
[6] E, II, prop. 13, lemma 7.
[7] E, II, prop. 7.
[8] E, I, prop. 16.
[9] Roth, *Spinoza*, p. 68.

tion, such as is envisaged by the Unity of Science program—a single, massive, tautological statement of every relationship and the formula of every existent.[10]

Spinoza thinks of extended substance as indivisible and undifferentiated, and added that it is also infinite in extent and "solid"—there is no vacuum, no interstices. Although Spinoza has been called a materialist, "extension" seems to mean to him "energy field" rather than "inert mass." [11] It is noteworthy that he adopted both the Averroistic unity of all mind and the Parmenidean unity of all body, only to merge both into the unity of Substance.

Neither substance nor its attributes are directly experienced; the world we know is made up of modes, modifications of substance. Modes are not illusory or unreal; they are the only way in which reality expresses itself; substance stripped of its modes would not exist. Yet modes are not "pieces" of substance, as energy fields are not a sum of parts, are not things, but situations or processes.

Of the single complex system which constitutes reality, outside of which nothing exists, it may be said that it is the cause of all that happens and that, given the principle of complete determinism and the absence of external influence, it must be considered to act freely out of the necessities of its own character. The less complex modal systems which we are and know are less free in that they exist among competing systems and as parts of more comprehensive systems.

The word "character," or "nature," here has little relation to classical or medieval concepts of natural law or final cause. When Spinoza says that each thing acts, when unhindered, out of the necessities of its own nature, he means that each thing has a characteristic way of acting which expresses its internal organization; the nature of a thing is completely ex-

<hr>

[10] TdIE, p. 15; McKeon, pp. 18, 162; Hampshire, p. 47.
[11] Wolf, Correspondence, p. 62; Pollock, Spinoza: His Life and Philosophy, pp. 102–103; E, I, props. 13–15.

pressed by its actual behavior in the absence of interference. Thus no event or activity can be called unnatural.[12]

Each thing that exists, then, considered in isolation from other things, has a set of behavior patterns, rules of its nature. Its existence or action in accordance with its nature may be called its freedom,[13] as its behavior in accordance with alien patterns may be called its passivity, or bondage.[14] Simple examples do not come readily to mind: iron exhibits magnetic characteristics in its pure state but not as ferrous oxide, a compounded thing to which iron contributes at the cost of its freedom of expressing itself as it would in isolation. Although it is a more complex matter, it may be more intuitively clear and relevant to the discussion of Spinoza's politics which follows if we consider the difference between a man acting out of full knowledge of the circumstances of his action and for ends really valuable to him,[15] and another man, performing the same acts but for another's purposes, or out of confusion, anger, ignorance, or conditioning. Yet the example of ferrous oxide, although not used by him, may have a use in clarifying Spinoza's idea that systems may not only lose their "freedom" to each other but may also, in so doing, produce a third, superordinate system. Since all finite systems are in collision in some sense, this third system is in turn part of some larger system, and so on until we arrive once more at the final system of Nature, or at God.[16] No hierarchy of systems is implied; Spinoza is here neither anticipating Spencer nor relapsing into neo-Platonism.

Nothing, except Nature, exists in isolation or free from the interference of other things, and so nothing, even man, is other than mostly passive. Only Nature, or God, can be said to act with complete freedom, out of the necessities of its own

[12] TTP, XVI, 125.
[13] E, IV, prop. 59; E, IV, App. 2; TP, II, par. 11.
[14] TP, II, par. 5; E, IV, prop. 35.
[15] E, IV, prop. 59; E, IV, prop. 2; E, II, def. 4.
[16] E, II, prop. 13, lemma 7.

nature, solely by the rules of its own organization.[17] Yet self-determination, although the ultimate in freedom, the very definition of freedom, is nevertheless determination and so not even God has free will.[18] Free will, defined as action without a cause, is in any case inconceivable. The appearance of fortuity, accident, or uncaused decision is an appearance only, the result of our incomplete apprehension of causes.

Another deduction from the ontological proof of "God" is the elimination of final causes, of teleology, and therefore of immanent value in nature.[19] Nature, complete by definition, cannot be dominated by an alien principle and so moved toward an end, nor can it be thought that a better or more complete state is possible for it than that in which it exists at any one time. This view does not run counter to evolutionary theories of the adjustment of organisms to environment, which adjustments may be evaluated by men according to their scale of utilities. It does contradict any theory of evolution which attempts to demonstrate "progress" in any sense other than that men approve the results of change. Spinoza speaks of Nature as perfect,[20] meaning complete, but never as good.

All things, then, iron, tree, man, are more or less complex modes arranged in certain ways which constitute their being. If the arrangement is distorted beyond some critical limit, the thing as such perishes. The amount of force required to destroy it is the measure of its power of self-preservation. We may perhaps best understand Spinoza here if we think of him as attempting to synthesize three principles: the first law of thermodynamics, applied to all extended bodies; homeostasis, applied to organic creatures; and the "instinct of self-preservation," as understood to apply to man and animals.

---

[17] E, I, prop. 17; E, IV, Pref.; TTP, XVI, 125; TP, II, par. 3.
[18] TP, II, par. 7; TTP, III, 53–55; TdIE, p. 32; cf., Augustine *City of God* xii. 5.
[19] TTP, XVI, 127; TdIE, p. 6; E, IV, Pref.; E, I, App.
[20] E, II, def. 6.

The important point for our purpose is that he thought that self-preservation was the first law of all beings.[21]

To recapitulate: Spinoza attempts to prove that the universe is a single and infinite system, that there *is* a universe, a cosmos, that it is known to us in two ways, as thought and as extension, and that everything in it is determined to act as it does by efficient causes only in the case of the modes of extended substance and by logical causes only in the case of the modes of substance conceived under the attribute of thought.[22] Spinoza uses these elements of a metaphysical system to solve those problems set forth in the last chapter. For example:

The reconciliation of God's goodness with the existence of evil is not a problem if we recognize that God is neither good nor bad but ethically neutral,[23] that evil is only a human term to describe that which men do not desire for themselves.

No reconciliation of God's foreknowledge with man's free will is necessary; neither God nor man has free will; "God's foreknowledge" is not a thought in the mind of a heavenly being, it is the fact that in a determined cosmos, the future is implicit in the present.

God's relation to the universe is understood when we see that God is himself the universe. He is so in two senses: as *natura naturans*, "nature naturizing," he is the active principle of the organization of all things,[24] as *natura naturata*, "nature naturized," he is that which is organized.[25]

The lines of solution to other theological problems should now be evident. Evident also should be the validity of the use of the word "subversive" to describe Spinoza's employment of

---

[21] TTP, XVI, 125; TP, II, par. 6.
[22] Randall, pp. 439, 442, 540, puts the matter differently.
[23] TTP, XVI, 125; E, I, prop. 33.
[24] TTP, III, 53: "By the guidance of God I mean the fixed and immutable order of nature, or the coherent system of natural things"; TTP (Dover), VI, 83.
[25] TTP (Dover), I, 25.

previously existing frameworks of thought. It is not possible in this short space to convey an adequate impression of the profundity and sweep of his destructive analysis of traditional theology or to show why his concept of God has been thought to be the most internally consistent yet brought forward. It is true that his final notion of God's nature bears little relation to that of the theologians and none to that of popular belief, yet both logic and genuine religious feeling have often in the past pushed the idea of God very close to that held by Spinoza.[26]

This *"Deus sive Natura"* has no interest in or even special knowledge of the fate of man;[27] he has no free will,[28] or will at all,[29] but is completely determined by his own nature to do and to be all that which he does and is.[30] It may be asked whether one who both does all and yet is all that is done can really do anything. Spinoza has been described as a pantheist, though not of the vulgar sort that asserts that each bit of matter or each finite idea is literally a fragment of God. Would he not more accurately be called, in agreement with the judgment of his contemporaries, an atheist?[31] An eighteenth-century rumor[32] has it that an early version of the *Ethics* contained the word "nature" wherever the word "God" now appears, and there are good historical reasons, as well as a great deal of internal textual evidence, for the belief that "God" for Spinoza was a completely appeasive term,[33] that it was used only to mislead potential persecutors and to mollify

[26] Santayana, Introduction to *Spinoza's Ethics and de Intellectus Emendatione*, p. xxii.

[27] Wolf, *Correspondence*, Ep. 23, pp. 190–91.

[28] TTP (Dover), VI, 83; E, I, prop. 32; E, I, prop. 33; Hubbeling, p. 27.

[29] E, I, n. 17; TTP, IV, 77; Wolf, *Correspondence*, Ep. 56, p. 287.

[30] TTP, IV, 83; TP, II, par. 7.

[31] Bayle, p. 291: "I think he is the first who reduced Atheism to a system."

[32] Deborin, p. 102.

[33] Wolfson, I, 177: "Bear in mind that Spinoza's God is not the God of traditional theology, that his 'God' is merely an appeasing term for the most comprehensive principle of the universe."

those who might be receptive to his way of thinking if not frightened off at the outset. Similarly, it could be argued that Spinoza's training and his method of working within older systems of thought led him to use the word "God" after it had for him lost all its original meaning. Yet there is a sense in which those who speak of Spinoza as a God-intoxicated man do not necessarily completely misunderstand him. For the moment we may suggest that the doubt as to whether we shall consider Spinoza an atheist—and it cannot completely be resolved—arises not so much from his own ambiguity as from the ambiguities inherent in the topic.[34] Spinoza certainly believed in *his* God, and he might have retorted to those who called him atheist because he did not believe in theirs [35] that the settlement of the question must await their giving as lucid an account of the object of their belief.[36]

Spinoza established his own reputation by publishing an uncritical exposition of the philosophy of Descartes. That philosophy, as he made clear, was not his own and when he later opposed it he did so not by direct criticism but by the presentation of an alternative. Some possible incoherencies and inadequacies of Cartesianism have been suggested in the preceding chapter. Spinoza's doctrine of substance and attributes was intended to eliminate dualism by showing that extension and thought are equally expressions of reality and to establish the validity of reason by showing both its independence of experience and its exact mirroring of the extended world.

Perhaps most interesting for us, today, is the view of Spinoza's metaphysics as a system for the validation of the results of

[34] The recent "God is dead" discussions illustrate the complexities of the subject; DeVries, p. 128: "It is the final proof of God's omnipotence that he need not exist in order to save us."
[35] TTP (Dover), XIII, 178: Because belief without understanding is impossible, and only a few understand, most men are actually atheists.
[36] TTP (Dover), II, 27; TTP, VI, 87.

scientific effort, of science itself.[37] Seventeenth-century scientific literature displays great confusion of method and outlook.[38] The principle of the uniformity of nature had no general acceptance among scientists themselves; explanations that were based on an implicit doctrine of final causes, or that resorted to the mere verbalism of "occult qualities," were common. Perhaps a greater hindrance to the progress of science than the primitive state of apparatus and basic concepts was the absence of a metaphysical view of reality by which science could be shown to be possible, valid, and valuable. Now, when the attempt to formulate a rigorous scientific method has become a new scholasticism, scientism a new superstition, and the pursuit of science both bureaucratized and morally suspect, it should be interesting to reconsider the outlook and program of Spinoza to discover how science was originally understood.[39]

Spinoza wrote before the great Newtonian synthesis had captured the imagination of men and changed their picture of the nature of the physical world. Bacon, Galileo, Hobbes, and Descartes had all preceded Spinoza, but only in his system are all the problems of a scientific metaphysics treated with any degree of adequacy,[40] not only from the narrow standpoint of

[37] Collingwood, p. 6.

[38] Wolf, *A History of Science*, II, 629–30, 651–52.

[39] Hampshire, p. 79: "It must again be noticed how astonishingly Spinoza, in his modal system of extension, has anticipated in outline the concepts and theoretical methods of modern science. If (as is sometimes suggested) metaphysical systems or cosmologies are to be judged as programmes or drafts in outline of the structure of a future science, it is not too much to claim that Spinoza, at least in his account of Nature as Extension, was less incomplete in his anticipations than any other philosopher . . . It was not until the end of the last century that his three conceptions (a) of motion-and-rest as the essential and universal feature of the extended world, and (b) of ultimate particles as centres of energy, and (c) of configurations of these ultimate particles forming relatively self-maintaining systems, were seen to correspond with actually used scientific concepts."

[40] Pollock, *Spinoza: His Life and Philosophy*, pp. 83, 147; Randall, p. 434: Spinoza "was the only man who really believed in the new science," "he saw its implications as no contemporary did."

physical inquiry, but with regard to the whole spectrum of man's interests, including the social and the ethical.[41]

The necessary metaphysical (not practical) assumptions for science are: That the world it studies be one—otherwise there would be two or more incompatible sciences, or one science subject to all manner of arbitrary exceptions; that nature act in a uniform manner [42] and, as extended, by efficient causation only [43]—or valid generalizations would be impossible. All independent variables must be excluded, not only miracles and the swerving of atoms but, for the sake of the unborn science of psychology, human free will. Nature itself, and man as a part of nature must be studied objectively

[41] Spinoza's philosophy of science has been the subject of considerable controversy in the last generation, partly because of the obscurity of his writings in some critical regards, partly because the issues, particularly the question of the relation of mathematical to empirical truth, are yet in dispute. At one place, TP, XIV, 123, he says that "philosophy is based on common notions, and must be built on the study of nature alone"; at Epistle 6 (Wolf, Correspondence, p. 94), the contrary view seems to be taken, namely that knowledge is only of the whole, or of a whole. McKeon discusses this question at length at pp. 115, 119, 130, 139–56, 168, and 228–29. Other references are: TTP, V, 99–101; TTP (Dover), II, 28; TdIE, pp. 11, 13; Bidney, p. 286; Hampshire, pp. 46–48: "This doctrine of the essential identity of the Creator and his Creation, so far from being mystical and anti-scientific in intention, leads logically to the conclusion that every single thing in the Universe necessarily belongs to, or falls within, a single, intelligible, causal system . . . This so-called pantheistic doctrine can in fact be fairly represented as the metaphysical expression of the ideal or programme of a unified science, that is, of a completed science which would enable every natural change to be shown as a completely determined effect within a single system of causes; everything must be explicable within a single theory. This ideal or programme has always fascinated theoreticians of science, and has been re-stated as a logical, and not metaphysical, thesis within the present century; a programme which could be intelligently expressed in the seventeenth century in metaphysical terms, as an *a priori* thesis about the creation and structure of the Universe, can intelligibly be expressed in this century in logical terms, as an *a priori* thesis about the structure of the language of science." The main burden of the charge against Spinoza's idea of the proper conduct and aim of science is that of excessive rationalism—excessive not in the sense of absolute falsity, but in the sense of premature synthesis. Seventeenth-century science was not ready for a Unified Field Theory.
[42] TTP (Dover), VI, 82.
[43] E, IV, Pref.; E, I, App.

and without the assumption of immanent value or purpose. The human mind must be shown capable of apprehending truth. This requires not only that the world be in fact structured in ways not beyond human comprehension, that is, that true and general statements about it be possible,[44] but also that the process of reasoning itself be internally coherent, that it be relevant to the world of experience, and that man be a creature who can reason.[45] Uniform and objective rules of evidence must be adopted. A logic of science, the setting up of rational criteria of truth, is intended here, as well as the rejection of appeals to authority.[46] The scientific enterprise itself must be shown to be worthwhile.[47] This is likely to be assumed without argument now, but it is perhaps the most important, historically, of the necessary assumptions. Man's study of the world and of himself must be conducted objectively, without immediate reference to value, if it is to be scientific, but the motivation for making the study is ethical in that it seeks something of value. The only thing that is valuable, so far as men are concerned, is the good of men. Science must therefore be understood to produce some good, and that good must be the welfare of men during their earthly existence.[48] It is further necessary to show that the importance of man's temporal welfare is not reduced to insignificance in comparison with a supposed future life to which his present life is but a prolegomenon.

Because Spinoza's metaphysics is directed to the validation of these postulates, we may well consider it a philosophy of science. By retaining the word "God" in his philosophic vocabulary, Spinoza was able to draw on the vast fund of analytic sophistication achieved in the course of centuries of theologi-

---

[44] TTP (Dover), Pref., p. 4.
[45] TTP (Dover), I, 14; TdIE, p. 34.
[46] TTP, V, 99; Wolf, *Correspondence*, Ep. 54, p. 277: "Let us, however, dismiss the authors and attack the question itself."
[47] TTP (Dover), I, 11; TdIE, p. 6.
[48] TdIE, p. 7.

cal disputation. Compared to that development, the new philosophies of science, even when done by a Bacon or a Descartes, were naive. Spinoza's translation of the conceptual apparatus and techniques of analysis, so painstakingly and brilliantly built up by generations of scholastics, into the secular idiom of a philosophy of science is an awe-inspiring intellectual accomplishment.

Spinoza's epistemology can be mentioned only cursorily. It is substantially the same as that of Plato's "divided line," although there is no reason to suppose that Spinoza was aware of the resemblance.[49] There are four types or levels of knowledge:[50] imagination, hallucination, or hearsay; opinion derived from ordinary experience; reasoned connections derived from assumptions; the certainty of direct intuition of reality. Spinoza admits that he has attained to very little of this fourth kind of knowledge; certainly he seems less open than is Plato to the charge of confusing intuitive certainty with the truth of intuition.[51] It is by the fourth kind of knowledge that we know, for example, that seven plus five is twelve; it is by the third kind, reasoned conclusion or recollection, that we know that 79 plus 55 is one hundred and twenty-four.[52]

In the *Ethics*, his major work, Spinoza presented his philosophy "in the manner of a mathematical proof." It is not necessary here to argue his intentions or attempt to discover the degree of his success. On the one hand, his philosophy is indeed of the sort that might, in principle, be demonstrated mathematically and there is much internal evidence that he

[49] TdIE, p. 8; E, II, prop. 40; Their ontologies were, of course, very different. For Plato, some "opinion" is uncertain knowledge because its object is itself incoherent. Spinoza admits incoherent thoughts, but not incoherent objects of thought.

[50] The differences between the epistemology of the TdIE and of the *Ethics* are not important here. The fourth kind of knowledge in the TdIE is identical with the third kind of the *Ethics*.

[51] TdIE, p. 9; TTP, V, 107; Pollock, *Spinoza: His Life and Philosophy*, pp. 140, 151.

[52] The third kind of knowledge can be false.

did make the attempt.[53] On the other hand, he used the same method in expounding the philosophy of Descartes, from which one might conclude that his purpose was not to achieve apodictic certainty but to gain maximum lucidity with minimum resort to rhetoric. His statement that he held, not the best, but the true philosophy, seems to indicate more certainty about his conclusions than about the means of reaching them.[54]

This distinction between "best" and "true" may serve to turn our attention from such matters as his probable failure to relate his definitions to an actual state of affairs, his apparent wavering on the status of universals, the puzzle of the relation of modes to substance, and so forth, to the question of whether his metaphysics may gain some credence as a working hypothesis. This in turn is a part of the larger question of the nature and function of metaphysical thought itself—a topic which is beyond the scope of this study.

[53] TTP (Dover), vii, 113; E, III, Pref.
[54] Wolf, *Correspondence*, Ep. 76, p. 352; Duff, p. 4: "Probably he did regard it as a more directly convincing mode of statement rather than as a more cogent kind of proof."

IV

Human Nature

❖

Man a Part of Nature

THE extended world of Descartes was a determined world; stones, animals, and the bodies of men were machines or parts of machines. God was distinctly outside of the world, although he had created it and intervened in it, occasionally, to perform miracles, and at every moment to sustain it. Within this world, but not of it, is the mind and free will of man. Cartesianism thus contains two basic ingredients, or independent variables. We have seen how Spinoza assimilated the idea of God to a naturalistic, monistic, outlook; it remains to show how he sees man's place in the world.

Again and again, Spinoza asserts that man is an integral part of nature, that he is not a kingdom within a kingdom.[1] In no sense is man to be set apart from the rest of nature: the structure of his body, his actions, reveries, preferences and errors, and even his philosophy, are as much a part of the natural order as is any material object or organic being, as completely determined, though in more complex ways, as they. This is as thoroughgoing a naturalism as can be. Spinoza never wavers from it or from its further implications. The rational man is in no other case in this regard than is the irrational man.[2]

[1] E, III, Pref.; E, IV, prop. 4; Wolf, *Correspondence*, Ep. 30, p. 205.
[2] TP, II, par. 5.

Mind and Body: Reason and Passion

Yet, within the concourse of nature, man is unique, as far as we know, in that he is both a thinking and an extended creature.[3] He is both, it should be emphasized, not as a casual collocation of incompatibles, but as a finite modal unity which can be conceived under both of the known attributes.[4] Spinoza's thought here is difficult and possibly incomplete; various commentators have found it possible to argue that he has, in this matter, opted for the superiority of the mind, and may therefore be termed an idealist, or that, because "the mind is the idea of the body," [5] he is really a materialist. Neither view seems to meet the conditions of his metaphysics, where the intention that all attributes be considered complementary and equal is clear. Certainly Spinoza holds neither the materialist view that thought is epiphenomenal nor the idealist view that extended bodies are intellectual constructs. Some resemblance in his thought to that of Aristotle may be detected: for both, the soul is the form of the body, although for Spinoza the mind of man has an orientation toward, or inherent potentiality for grasping, rational truth which is closer to the position of Plato.

As embodied mind or minded body, man is yet a part of the natural order. As a mode of extended substance he is completely a part of the endless chain of determined events; as a mode of substance under the attribute of thought, his adequate ideas are part of the equally determined logical order of thought. Man is a thinking animal; he is an animal capable of thinking the thoughts of the world order; that is, he can grasp objective relationships.[6] Between potentiality and performance, however, lies a gap.

The Passions. Man is a complex unity, characterized as are

[3] E, IV, App. 26; E, IV, App. 2.
[4] Saw, p. 113.
[5] E, II, prop. 13.
[6] E, II, prop. 7: "The order and connection of ideas is the same as the order and connection of things"; E, II, ax. 2: "Man thinks."

all such unities, by a drive toward self-preservation.[7] Insofar as he is considered as extended body, this drive is expressed by the passions. "Desire," the desire for self-preservation, is the general form of the passions. Most, if not all, of the events in life have some bearing, real or imagined, remote or immediate, on the satisfaction of desire; the experience of these events is therefore attended by feelings of pleasure or of pain. Pleasures and pains are accompaniments of changes in the condition of a man rather than continuing states. At this level of discussion, therefore, Spinoza is in agreement with Hobbes that there is no final good for man, that pleasure accompanies only the transition from one state to a desired other state, whereas pain accompanies the transition to a less desired or undesired state.[8] Almost all of Book III of the *Ethics* is devoted to the deduction of the commonly named passions according to this scheme. Love, for example, is pleasure associated with the idea of an external cause;[9] hatred is pain similarly associated. The passions are natural phenomena[10] and should be regarded as "properties which belong to it [the mind] in the same way as heat, cold, storm, thunder and the like belong to the nature of the atmosphere."[11] Man cannot be conceived as without passions;[12] they are the source of the energy necessary to every action or thought. Passion is not bad in itself, nor even in relation to men's interests, except insofar as it hinders thought.[13] Further, every action and the occurrence of every thought (but not its content) and mental image are the result of the victory of the strongest passion operating at the time.[14]

[7] E, III, prop. 6; E, III, prop. 57.
[8] E, III, sch. 11; E, III, def. 3; Aristotle *Politics* 1267b.
[9] E, III, prop. 51; McKeon, at p. 251, sees Spinoza's deduction of the passions as mechanistic, "not unlike the laws that underlie the transference of motion."
[10] E, IV, n. 57.
[11] TP, I, par. 4.
[12] E, IV, cor. 4.
[13] E, V, prop. 9.
[14] E, IV, props. 7, 14, 16.

Because the passions are solely directed, however blindly, toward self-preservation, and because man acts only on the basis of some passion, however modified by rational considerations, it might be thought that men's actions would be in fact more self-preserving than they seem to be.[15] Two considerations are relevant here. The first is that man is a finite creature, living among other finite creatures, human and not, and clearly without power to extend his life indefinitely or even, because the determined chain of events is not known to him, to ward off accident. Second, because of man's egocentric predicament, because his body is both a screen between his understanding and the extended world and the sole source of information about that world, he suffers from a simple lack of data as to what is indeed self-preserving. Man's passion to preserve himself is only weakly effective, therefore, because it is misdirected; the unenlightened passions react passively to immediate stimuli; [16] each passion seeks its own end without regard to the whole personality. This is the essence of the plight of man, that he must pursue his interests on the basis of inadequate information, that what true information he does have is subject to interference, the static of the passions.[17]

Reason. Man's essence, which he shares with all modal entities, is the desire to preserve himself; the essence peculiar to him as a man is his capacity for understanding, that is, his capacity to use reason as means both to know what preservation is and to attain it.[18] Several points in this matter are noteworthy:

Man's rationality is a finite mode of the intellect of God,[19] that is, it is a partial representation of the abstract formula of the universe. Just as nature, thinking, is the complete counterpart of nature as extended, so we may think of man's modal

---

[15] Marcuse, pp. 11–12.
[16] E, IV, prop. 44; E, IV, prop. 60.
[17] E, IV, prop. 62; E, V, prop. 36.
[18] E, IV, prop. 26.
[19] TTP (Dover), I, 14; Aristotle *Nicomachean Ethics* 1177b.

intellect as representing, although incompletely and with some confusion, the formula of his own body in particular and of the universe in general.[20] Our stock of true, "adequate," ideas may not be large,[21] but each of them is not merely correspondent to a fact or to a general truth, but is part of, not a reflection of, truth itself, constitutive of rather than "about" a fact. For us to have true and adequate ideas is for us to participate in, to be understandable in terms of, to be ourselves part of God as apprehended under the attribute of thought.[22] It should be noted that the mind is not the brain, nor any kind of object or faculty, but is the actual understanding itself, operating with concepts, not with images or feelings.[23] It is of primary importance to the understanding of Spinoza's political and ethical thought that this point be clear. As Duff puts it: "This union of the mind with God, or with Nature as a whole, is the essential condition of all moral goodness and of all political unity."[24] The union of the mind with the whole of nature is at best occasional. The minimal claim made by Spinoza is that we at times understand what is going on about us; the denial of the possibility of such a union or of the meaningfulness of the concept is the denial that, for instance, mathematical systems have *any* relevance to the data of experience.

What goes on in a man's head is doubly determined. The chain of sensations, passions, and images is determined by the chain of events in the world of extension and by the psychological laws of association, but when man enters into the world of the understanding, he is subject to the laws of thought: ". . . it is plain that our mind, in so far as it under-

[20] TdIE, p. 6: "human weakness . . . cannot match in its thoughts the regular order of nature."
[21] TdIE, p. 9.
[22] E, II, prop. 34; E, II, prop. 1; TTP (Dover), I, 14; TdIE, pp. 15, 25, 28, 34.
[23] E, II, props. 48, 49; TdIE, pp. 31–33, 40.
[24] P. 13.

stands, is an eternal mode of thinking, which is determined by another eternal mode of thinking, and this other by a third, and so on to infinity." [25] Although the lines of causation are different, I am equally determined to undertake the study of geometry and to acquiesce in the truth of a particular proposition.

Of the truths of reason we may say further that they are timeless, not subject to modal contingency, and true of nature as a whole.[26]

It is not enough and is possibly misleading, to say that man has a capacity for reasoning. Spinoza's psychology is a drive, not a faculty psychology; the resemblance of his view to that of earlier analysts of human nature, particularly the Stoics, ceases here. As desire is the basic passion, so it is also at the root of rationality; man's essence is the desire to understand [27] but reason is itself a passion.[28] Spinoza here rejects what had become an almost standard philosophical bifurcation of man into contending rational and passionate elements.[29] The ends of reason are not fundamentally different from but are enlightened versions of the ends of the passions. The goal of man as a rational creature is preservation through the understanding, preservation of the understanding, and preservation of oneself as a coherent being. Spinoza calls this goal the intellectual love of God, or freedom; the term more commonly used now is personal autonomy. The intellect operates in two distinguishable ways: it is the scout or slave of the passions, although as the slave of the master passion for self-preservation it can successfully divert the destructive demands of many particular passions; and, insofar as it is itself a part of the attribute of thought, it can be the independent leader of the total personality toward ends not in conflict with but

[25] E, V, n. 40.
[26] E, V, prop. 29.
[27] E, IV, props. 26, 61.
[28] E, III, prop. 58; E, III, prop. 2, note.
[29] Bidney, p. 282, to the contrary.

incomprehensible to the simple passions. The distinction must
not be taken to be a division; it corresponds to the ordinary
and far from exact line we draw between motives of self-
interest and of enlightened self-interest.

Since reason is a kind of passion, its satisfactions or defeats
are accompanied by pleasure or pain as in the case of the other
passions.[30] Hobbes also allowed the existence of intellectual
pleasures but in his thought they seem but refinements of
more gross satisfactions; for Spinoza they are tied to the preservation of man as a thinking being, concomitants of his steps
toward the achievement of freedom.

Spinoza sees conflict everywhere, from the level of the
simplest entities competitively struggling to maintain themselves to the political life of man. Each man is himself the
arena of unending struggle. The simple passions contend, as
when I choose between two dishes in a restaurant, only one of
which I can afford. The intellect and the passions contend, as
in the case of my craving for a certain food which I know will
make me sick. Intellect here is the scout of the passion for
self-preservation. The desire for the food is also a passion for
self-preservation, but misconceived. The fear of the stomach
ache is a rational fear, in that it follows the calculation of
probable consequences; Spinoza recommends heeding it not
because it has some dignity or moral force derived from its
rationality but because it directs me toward a greater happiness or a lesser pain. Reason, which is to say the informed
passions, does not always determine the event; the indigestible
food is sometimes eaten despite my knowledge of the consequences.[31] I may see the better, yet follow the worse. The
power of reason over passion is the power to confront a
passion with the effective means for its fulfillment, with a yet
stronger passion for an alternative good, or with a rationally
arrived at fear of the unwanted consequences attending the

[30] E, III, Pref.; Aristotle *Nichomachean Ethics* 1178a.
[31] E, IV, prop. 16.

satisfaction of the passion. We may observe both that reason is commonly very weak, and yet that it is very persistent—its small voice is easily lost in the roar of the competing simple passions but it says always the same thing and often prevails.[32]

Even the extreme case of the power of reason to choose death above "dishonor"[33] does not refute the assertion that self-preservation is the aim of reason, which

demands that every man should love himself, should seek that which is useful to him,—I mean, that which is really useful to him, should desire everything which really brings man to greater perfection, and should, each for himself, endeavour as far as he can to preserve his own being.[34]

This question will be treated of at length later in this chapter; a condensed statement here may be helpful. The achievement of greater understanding is the achievement of greater autonomy, of actual being. If by "dishonor" we mean the voluntary renunciation of what inner coherence one has attained, the loss of actual being or, as it is put nowadays, the loss of that coherence called identity, then the choice of death as the alternative may be rational. "Personality" also means "mask" or "role"; a passion to maintain it is derived from a basic dependence on the opinion of others. Spinoza is not thinking of this superficial and false self-consciousness, but of the personal integrity of someone who has found himself as a limited but essentially autonomous person.

Reason, then, is directed toward the interest of man,[35] a creature whose peculiar essence is the desire to understand, whose true interest is the attainment of rationality. Therefore, given utility as the standard of value, good or evil for man is the name for what helps or hinders him from arriving at

[32] E, V, prop. 10.

[33] E, IV, prop. 72. Some readers may find amusement in the current necessity for putting "dishonor" in quotation marks.

[34] E, IV, prop. 18, note; *pace* Bidney, p. 139.

[35] TTP, XVI, 127; TP, II, par. 8.

rationality.[36] A man's virtue, that is to say, his power,[37] is most significantly measured by the extent of his understanding; the most rational man is the strongest, and so the freest, man.[38] This position may seem overly intellectualistic: for all the truth we may sometimes find in Plato's doctrine that "knowledge is virtue," yet "knowledge" is a complex concept, including such matters as synapses, physical orientations, and reality-centered characterological configurations; much of our knowledge has not been or cannot usefully be reduced to propositional form. Bidney, however, does not believe that Spinoza has fallen into the intellectualistic fallacy:

> Plato had said: All virtue is knowledge. Francis Bacon added: All knowledge is power. Spinoza concluded: Therefore all virtue is power. Spinoza accepts the Platonic doctrine that virtue is knowledge but interprets knowledge in the Baconian sense of efficient power.[39]

Human Nature

Spinoza's understanding of human nature is important to us, here, because his political theory is, he says, derived from a correct understanding of the nature of man,[40] a claim made also by Hobbes and Machiavelli.

Is Spinoza entitled to speak of a "human nature"? The phrase has come into some disrepute in reaction to its use in connection with teleological and religious views of the world and by shallow moralizers. His use of the phrase seems unexceptionable. "Human nature" for him implies neither faculty psychology nor natural law; it is not a magic bag from which he pulls forth whatever he needs to complete his system. Its components are clearly labeled and put together before our

---

[36] E, IV, prop. 27; Aristotle *Politics* 1252a.
[37] The classical and Machiavellian overtones of "virtue" as here used are noteworthy. In all three cases the word may be translated as "excellence."
[38] TP, III, pars. 6, 7.
[39] P. 283.
[40] TP, I, pars. 4, 7; TP, III, par. 18; Aristotle *Nichomachean Ethics* 1102a.

eyes; they do not differ essentially from those of modern psychology. It is not used as a normative concept; we are not urged to conform to it. There is, admittedly, a seeming ambiguity in Spinoza's use of the phrase "human nature": men are said to act freely when they act out of their own nature, that is, out of their human essence, their understanding. Yet, at other times, man's nature is seen not as his essence but as his existential plight—as when Spinoza says that for a politics to be based on human nature it must be based on the assumption that men have little actual understanding. There is never any difficulty in gathering from the context which meaning is intended.

Spinoza's assertion of a primary drive toward self-preservation, although suggested by experience, is to be understood as a deduction from his metaphysics. In the further development of his theory of human nature, however, particularly in the deduction of the passions, although he continues the form of the geometrical demonstration, his psychology is more evidently dependent upon observation. For example, the struggle to survive is a struggle of individuals and each man must be understood to pursue his own advantage to the exclusion of any interest in that of others.[41] Yet, because men are influenced more by their imaginations than by reason, and because pleasure is the result of a rising opinion of ourselves, which in turn depends in great part upon our apprehension of the opinion others hold of us, it follows that one of man's major objectives is the gaining of the good opinion of others, and so he is ambitious.[42] This is a psychology in that it accounts for the existence of the passion of ambition; it is an ethic in that ambition is shown to rest upon a misapprehension as to what is actually valuable to us.[43]

Spinoza's theory of human nature includes the theses, which

[41] TP, VII, par. 4; TdIE, p. 4.
[42] TP, VIII, par. 6.
[43] This last clause is anticipatory of the next section of this chapter.

can only be noted in passing, that the same laws of mental association apply to all men, that there are certain true ideas which can be held by all men, and that human nature is unchanging.[44] The arguments for these statements are lengthy and their apparently unverifiable character is striking; it is suggested that we accord them the same suspension of judgment allowed, with an eye to a possible heuristic value, to any preliminary set of axioms.

The theory is very general, sufficiently so to permit Spinoza to adopt, within it, the Machiavellian view that men are to a high degree socially plastic; "citizens are made, not born." [45] In the main, and with very few exceptions, even the mature beliefs and assumptions of men are the creation of family, social, and political training.[46]

Good and Evil

Man's nature cannot in itself be called good or bad. As a natural phenomenon, it is outside the range of evaluation. As itself the ground of human evaluation, it cannot be judged by the values which arise out of it.[47] Spinoza does, at very many places, speak disparagingly of the mass of men, but he is at those places using accepted social criteria of goodness and badness, assessing, as does Machiavelli, the likelihood that people will live up to their professed standards. His motive is realism, not cynicism or moral condemnation; he means to avoid the useless contemplation of utopias based on false understandings of the possibilities of human nature and to show that practical political proposals must and can be based on human nature as it actually is.

Spinoza's position on human nature is moderately

[44] TTP, IV, 67; E, II, prop. 38; TTP (Dover), XII, 166.
[45] TP, V, par. 2; TTP, III, 57; E, III, def. 27; Machiavelli, Discourses, III, Ch. 43, p. 575.
[46] TTP, XVII, 179-81: "laws and customs, are the only factors which can give a people a particular temperament, a particular nature, and lastly particular beliefs."
[47] TP, II, par. 6; TP, VII, par. 12.

pessimistic.[48] Aside from his belief that the lot of ordinary men can be much improved by an adjustment of political mechanisms, he thinks that "salvation" is possible, that individual men can arrive at a considerable degree of freedom, and that there is no necessary limit to the number of men who can do so: "The endeavor of the better part of ourselves is in harmony with the order of nature as a whole." [49] He does not consider the possibility that human nature is out of harmony with the nature of things in general or that men live in a world which is so made as necessarily to defeat their aspirations, although his general metaphysics appear not necessarily to rule out such possibilities.[50]

Spinoza notes that men use the terms "good" and "evil" to describe those things or events which tend to gratify or frustrate their desires.[51] Except for the qualification that these desires must be for what is really needed, if their objects are to be called good, he wants to add nothing to the operational definition. For men in bondage to the unenlightened passions, or for philosophers who do not distinguish levels of ends relative to a distinct concept of human nature, Spinoza will thus appear to be an ethical relativist. He is not, for he understands man's desires to be fixed in their general form by his essence and circumstances; good and evil, if only for men, are objectively given. The good is what helps, evil is what hinders men from arriving at freedom.

[48] E, V, props. 4, 10. By "pessimistic" I mean the view that man in his original state is "bad" (in Machiavelli's sense of that word at *Discourses*, I, Ch. 3), that is, unsocial and lacking in native virtue or excellence. The moderately pessimistic view is that man is bad but improvable, as contrasted with the optimistic view of human nature, a view which does not appear in a fully developed form until Rousseau and which implies a present deterioration, socially caused, from an original excellence.

[49] E, IV, App. 32.

[50] Santayana, *Dominations and Powers*, pp. 180–81: "Thus the formal perfection of the universe, as completely expressing its own nature and laws, covers a moral chaos, in which the vital nature or law of each thing is defeated and turned into a maimed and monstrous caricature of what that thing was capable of becoming."

[51] E, IV, Pref.

Spinoza's definition of good is therefore utilitarian [52] in contrast to Plato's opinion that the good which man desires is a good independent of, though congruent with, human advantage. Both philosophers agree, however, in denying that "man is the measure of all things" in the sense that each man in his decisions determines, for himself, the whole range of values, or that some or even all men establish what is good for themselves by consensus.[53] Both agree that the wise man is the measure;[54] a fundamental similarity of their philosophies could hardly be more succinctly stated.

Hobbes, on the other hand, agrees with Spinoza in denying the transcendent character of the good,[55] but in saying that the good for each man is what he desires, Hobbes appears to fall into contradiction with his own principle of the primacy of self-preservation.[56]

The good, then, is objectively given to man but is not transcendent; it is the useful; it is that which preserves and is therefore accompanied by pleasure. Each man, by natural right, may judge of what is good and bad for himself, but he may be and often is mistaken; not all that is done by right is done well.[57] "By natural law I am bound to choose the lesser evil" [58]—as I see it.

Natural Right

"Rights" and "duties" are usually held to be correlative concepts. A chapter will be devoted to Spinoza's argument on political obligation; here we consider his theory of natural right, on which there has been some confusion.

In its ordinary moral sense, "right" has no place in Spinoza's

[52] E, IV, prop. 20; Spinoza, *The Short Treatise*, p. 145.
[53] TP, V, par. 1; Plato *Cratylus* 386 A ff.
[54] TdIE, p. 6; E, IV, Pref.
[55] Hobbes, *Leviathan*, p. 63.
[56] See Chapter IX, below.
[57] TP, VI, par. 3.
[58] TTP, XVI, 131.

naturalistic, nonteleological view of a cosmos in which even "God" is an ethically neutral term. It would have been possible for Spinoza to have said simply that man has no rights; he does not do so. Instead, he equates right with power. The basic statement is: "Each thing in nature has as much right from nature as it has power to exist and act." [59] As for man, "I start from the natural rights of the individual, which are co-extensive with his desires and power." [60]

This is perhaps the central statement in Spinoza's political thought; [61] if there is any point at which one could separate that thought from his metaphysics, it would be here, although only in the light of the metaphysics can the full force of the point be seen. Spinoza knew how critical was his natural right theory to his system; he spoke of it as being the principal distinction between his own political theory and that of Thomas Hobbes. [62]

Spinoza's employment of the phrase "natural right" is exact and consistent despite its difference from the customary usage. [63] Hobbes's use of the phrase has ethical overtones: my right to do all that is necessary for self-preservation is not equal to a right to do everything I can do; I have a right to do things which in fact I cannot do; I have no right to injure other men in cases where my own preservation is not involved. Hobbes arrived at his meaning of "right" within an ethical context; after excluding one by one all counterclaims, he finally arrives at the unlimited right to do all for survival. [64] Spinoza denies the separation of right from power: if I cannot

[59] TP, II, par. 3.
[60] TTP (Dover), Pref., p. 10; Aristotle *Politics* 1284a.
[61] TP, II, par. 18; TTP, XVI, 125, 139; TP, II, 267, 269, 279; E, IV, prop. 37; Vaughan, *Studies in the History of Political Philosophy*, I, 122.
[62] Wolf, *Correspondence*, Ep. 50, p. 269.
[63] Pufendorf (Vol. II, p. 162), is one of the few writers who have argued at length against Spinoza's "right equals might" thesis. The refutation which Pufendorf offers is based on a misapprehension of Spinoza's thought; the *Ethics* and the *Tractatus Politicus* had not yet been published.
[64] It must be admitted that there is no general agreement on this or on any other interpretation of the character of "right" in Hobbes's writings.

move my finger, I have no right to move it; if I can remove a slight annoyance by destroying the world, and I can destroy the world, I have a right to do it.

In a sense all the major ramifications of Spinoza's political thought are a deduction from his equivalence of right with power. For example: two men united have more right than either separately; my right over anything is limited to the kind of power I have over it—my right to my desk does not extend to making it eat grass; right is not limited to rational acts but extends to all that "appetite can suggest"; because men are weakest in the state of nature, they have least right there; power means any kind of power—military power, money power, intellectual power, the power of numbers; the power which is most useful to man is the power of the understanding;[65] the power of the state is the collective power of its members, and so varies with the extent to which it is actually collected. It also follows that the rights of one person are limited by the rights of another, not in the usual sense of a moral equilibrium, but in the novel sense of a physical equilibrium, the resultant of a parallelogram of forces. Rights have, so to speak, a marketplace rating. The world of the classical economists and of the group theorists is just one step further along.

Determinism and Ethical Freedom

Spinoza's reconciliation of determinism with ethical freedom is one of his most generally accepted contributions to the corpus of philosophical thought. As has been noted, Spinoza denies free will both to man and to God. Every motion or thought is completely the effect of the preceding state of affairs or is the logical consequence of a preceding thought.[66] Our subjective certainty of the freedom of our choice is but a reflection of our ignorance of the actual causes of that

[65] TP, II, pars. 5, 6, 8, 11, 13, 15; IV, par. 4; VII, par. 17.
[66] TP, III, pars. 6–7; TTP (Dover), III, 45.

choice.[67] This determinism is not to be confused with fatalism, a view which is incorrigibly teleological in that it sees the future as determining the present. Spinoza's determinism is radically "aimless"; the determination is from the past or is logical. We are determined to struggle for existence, but if we survive it is because we have struggled in an environment which permitted survival, not because we were fated to survive. Only because all is determined do the world, other men, and we ourselves have a character sufficiently stable to justify calculations and actions directed toward preservation. In a world which was undetermined, or to the degree to which it was undetermined, we should never have the coherency which makes us what we are; both action and thought would be anarchic, meaningless.[68]

Without free will there is, of course, no responsibility, and without responsibility there can be, it is thought, no ethics. How, then, can Spinoza both assert determinism and write an *Ethics*, a work which sets forth not merely a theory *about* ethics (that is to say, a sociological or psychological study of the genesis or function of ethical thinking), but an ethical theory?

Spinoza solved the problem by making a distinction and by changing the ground of the argument. All objects in nature are determined, but they are determined in two ways: passively as subject to passing circumstances,[69] and actively as subject to the requirements of their own nature,[70] which, in the case of man, means subjection to reason. This is the freedom which we have mentioned above, the ability to act out of the necessities for self-preservation of one's own essence.[71] The ground of the argument has changed from a difference

[67] Wolf, *Correspondence*, Ep. 56, p. 287, Ep. 58, p. 295, note at p. 451; E, I, prop. 33; Spinoza, "Cogita Metaphysica," appendix to *Principles of Descartes's Philosophy*, pp. 159–60.
[68] Hume, *Treatise*, p. 411.
[69] Wolf, *Correspondence*, Ep. 58, p. 294.
[70] TTP, IV, 83; Green, pp. 3, 4.
[71] TP, II, par. 7; E, I, def. 7.

between determinism and free will to a difference between passivity and activity; a distinction has been made between kinds of determinism.[72]

It is this concept of freedom as action originating wholly in the interest of the agent, and understood by him to be in his interest, which is contrasted with bondage, a state wherein the feeling of having acted is illusory, because the apparent actor is a mere transmitter of energies and interests foreign to him. The primitive, uncritical sense of freedom is that of the absence of hindrance to movement, and it is in this sense that Hobbes and many others use it. Spinoza arrives at his own meaning by analysis of this primitive meaning. What is a hindrance? What is an "I"? A prison wall or a broken leg hinder me, of course, in limiting the possibilities of movement. A pistol held at my head hinders me in quite another way, dramatically affecting the usual basis on which I make choices. A hindrance, then, is a limitation of power to do, or it is a curtailment of the area of choice. The question of the character of the agent is more interesting. When I act in confusion or ignorance, when I act as a culture-bound, conditioned, or hypnotized person, I evidently act for reasons not mine but those of another person, a society, a political system, or for no reason at all but merely in reaction to immediate stimuli.[73] Whether my behavior under these conditions is actually advantageous for myself, whether it is such as I should choose if

[72] Waelder, "Psychic Determinism and the Possibility of Prediction," p. 33, believes that two kinds of human behavior are predictable: (1) that which is guided by the mature ego, and (2) that in which the mature ego is practically excluded. Probably the furthest matter from Waelder's thought was the philosophy of Spinoza, but the parallel is striking, both in the distinction between men guided by reason and those who are victims of circumstance and in the distinction between logical and "physical" determination.

[73] This is an extension of Aristotle's definition of a slave as a living tool (*Politics* 1253b); Mill, p. 73: "A person whose desires and impulses are his own—are the expression of his own nature, as it has been developed and modified by his own culture—is said to have a character. One whose desires and impulses are not his own has no character, no more than a steam-engine has character."

I were fully aware of my interests and situation, or even whether it is of a kind such as will lead to my freedom in the future, are matters of great personal importance, but they have no immediate relevance to the question of my own freedom at the time.

It is man's essence to understand; man in acting out of his understanding is acting out of the necessities of his nature and this, by definition, is freedom. That man is free who understands both his interests and his circumstances. No man understands both completely and so no man is completely free,[74] yet men vary in the degree of freedom they have as well as in the spheres within which they have achieved it. I may be more free than you in one area, less in another. Spinoza's criterion of freedom is extremely rigorous in that even in the ideal case, never reached, of a person who has complete rationality and freedom, there is yet no responsibility in the moral sense, although such a person would be, in the common parlance, a "responsible person." The growth toward freedom is a change from random, incoherent determination from without to an equally complete determination from within. Given Spinoza's metaphysics, even this "within" is a kind of "without," for rational determination is conformity to the laws of thought, in the extended sense in which Spinoza understood them, rather than to the "laws" of a particular personality.[75]

Man's freedom, then, equals his power to know and act for his own interest and so can be seen as a special case of his natural right. Each man has a *right* to do all in his interest, as *he* sees it, that he can; but he is free only to the extent to which his idea of his interest actually corresponds to his real interest.[76]

[74] TP, II, par. 8.
[75] Spinoza's position must be distinguished from the Kantian acceptance of a rule of one's own making—see Kant, *Fundamental Principles of the Metaphysic of Morals*, p. 49.
[76] TP, II, par. 5; TP, II, par. 22; E, IV, prop. 24; Kohut, p. 481; ". . . for all that the persistent recovery of unconscious motivations and of rationali-

What are his real interests? Spinoza is not an ethical monist, not an ascetic; in addition to *the* Good, there are lesser goods which a man may wisely and advantageously pursue. Man has special but real interests corresponding to the varieties of his mundane situation and nature. He has an interest in peace and security, in nourishment, comfort and recreation, as well as in the pleasures of the intellect and in the achievement of the "intellectual love of God." All of these interests relate to self-preservation and none of them necessarily conflict with others. A piece of candy, a month in Florence—each can be good for us, both as a passing delight and as a contribution to our development.

Spinoza's own formulation is that man "can be called free only in so far as he has the power to exist and act in accord-

---

zation leads to is, under favorable circumstances, a wider and more vivid experience of freedom."

Brierly, p. 228: "It would seem that the ego is fulfilling its proper functions when it tries to make the most reasonable decision on the evidence before it, as if it were a responsible free agent. But the sounder the internal and external reality-sense of the ego, the better will it recognize the limiting conditions of its own choices and the more likely will it be to arrive at integrative, practicable, decisions. In relation to the total personality, the adequately realistic ego may well say with St. Paul: 'I live, yet not I.' "

Knight, p. 372: " . . . the healthy person has a combined feeling of freedom and inner compulsion. He feels that his course is determined by standards, beliefs, knowledge, aspirations that are an integral part of himself and he can do no other; yet at the same time he feels free. A decision or course of action that is in harmony with his character seems to carry with it the reward of a pleasurable sense of freedom. It is not easy to analyse the sense of freedom as it is used in this context, but it can be described more fully. In a negative sense it means absence of anxiety, of irrational doubt, and of those inhibitions and restrictions which paralyze both choice and action. In a positive sense it connotes feelings of wellbeing, of self-esteem, of confidence, of inner satisfaction based on successful use of one's energies for achievement that promotes the best interests of one's fellow men as well as one's own. It is part of the thesis of this essay that this kind of 'freedom' is experienced only by emotionally mature, well-integrated persons; it is the goal sought for one's patients in psychotherapy; and this freedom has nothing whatsoever to do with free will as a principle governing human behavior but is a subjective experience which is itself causally determined . . . The behavior of a well-integrated civilized person can be objectively assessed as 'free.' "

ance with the laws of human nature." [77] Freedom, "in accordance with the laws of human nature," is to seek and find understanding.[78] Because all men have the same essential nature, the same object is sought by each,[79] to the extent to which he is rational.

The basic meaning of freedom, then, is radically nonpolitical in Spinoza's thought. In the strict sense, freedom can neither be given nor withheld by the state; no matter what the circumstances, the free man can always do what is best for himself under those circumstances; [80] in the freest possible state, the subjectively unfree man is yet a slave.

Yet Spinoza's concept of freedom has political consequences. He quite agrees with Rousseau, for example, that the state may do well in forcing men to be free in the sense that the state may force upon a primitive or degenerate element within it those laws or institutions of civil society which are the conditions of the increased ability to pursue one's true interest, freedom.

A modern writer has remarked that "freedom is not to be understood as the illusory possession of an 'inner' spiritual realm compatible with actual enslavement, but as concrete individual liberty, i.e., the right to self-determination." [81] Although this is a sociological argument against a philosophical position and therefore at least slightly misses the issue, it has a certain force against the quietism of some religious thought and against the kind of Stoicism taught by Epictetus. It does not touch Spinoza's position. Few have been more aware than he of the degree of man's dependence on man, not only for safety and comfort but for help in the principal enterprise—the gaining of individual freedom. For Spinoza,

[77] E, IV, prop. 24; TP, II, par. 7.
[78] TTP, XVI, 135; TP, II, par. 11.
[79] TTP, III, 55; E, IV, prop. 36.
[80] TTP, XVI, 135; TTP, p. 247, n. 33: "A man can be free in any kind of state."
[81] Lichtheim, p. 27.

whoever seeks freedom for himself must necessarily seek it also for others, acting first on rational self-interest, and then from his understanding of the underlying unity of mankind. Far from being indifferent to political liberty, as we shall see, he advocates it as a most important means to individual freedom.

Self-Preservation and Salvation. Has Spinoza actually established a naturalistic ethic? Even if we allow that men arrive at different levels of freedom, does not a doctrine of psycho-physical determinism deprive even the freest of men of all claim to merit? Certainly. The incidence of exposure to those physical and intellectual influences which make possible the increase in freedom in an individual are completely beyond his control, as is his further use of those advantages. The parallel to Augustine's final doctrine of grace, determinism, and salvation is almost exact.[82]

Spinoza's ethical theory, then, is not a complex exhortation to do well, but an explanation of what doing well is; it is a complex piece of information, the intent of which is orientative. Our ability to grasp it or act on it is a matter of "chance" or "grace"; the source of our desire to act on it is our desire to preserve ourselves.

It is more than that. Our desire to preserve ourselves is not conditional on anything else and so statements which tell us how we may be preserved are not conditional but peremptory. To the extent to which we grasp the true ethic we are determined to follow it. As Plato put it, knowledge is virtue.

It is a strange desire to preserve oneself, it may be said,

[82] Deane, pp. 19, 22, 25; Froude, I, First Series, 361–64, where Spinoza is said to be "stating in philosophical language the extreme doctrine of Grace." The "extreme doctrine" is that a few men are saved by the arbitrary choice of God, that that choice cannot be influenced by any act on the part of men, that men have no free will. Spinoza's secular version of the doctrine is, of course, that a man arrives at the higher stages of knowledge, at freedom, by no merit or choice of his own. Those who are not fortunate in this way are "damned" to the emptiness of the life of the passions, the bondage, the slavery, of the unenlightened life.

which calls for "death before dishonor." [83] The matter is extraordinarily simple, and has been referred to briefly above. Approaching the matter genetically, we may cite the progression in a single life from the first elementary ordering of the passions in the face of reality, whereby a certain degree of physical integrity is achieved, to the adolescent revolt in favor of ego integrity in the social situation, to the adult acceptance of social responsibility, to the philosophical vision of the complete autonomy of the completely knowing mind, the inner transcendence of subjectivity, passion, and accident. The essence of the decision to choose death in certain contingencies is the decision not to sacrifice the degree of salvation—autonomy—one has attained merely to preserve, at a lower level, a physical existence. More, for where the pinch of incense offered the idol, or the facile equivocation, might seem not to endanger one's level of understanding, a new force comes into play—the conviction of the unity of interest that mankind, or that part of it which one has identified as mankind, has, and an unwillingness to betray it in one's own person.

Individualism

Individualism—which for the Hellenic Greeks was a kind of idiocy, for medieval culture was sinfulness and revolt against God, and for modern romantic thought has been prized, even as idiosyncrasy or eccentricity, as the heroic assertion of the single creative will—was, for the seventeenth-century political thinkers, a fact of life. It was the necessary beginning of social thinking, a problem, and a danger. The personal danger was "accidie" or alienation, the nightmare of Hamlet; the religious danger was the nightmare of every man a Pope in his own persecuting church; the political danger was the possibility of the assertion of individual conscience or caprice against the right of the state or of society, and the consequent anarchy. This is not the place to explore the many strands in

[83] E, IV, prop. 72; E, V, props. 38, 39.

history that led to the individualism of the seventeenth century; the implicitly holistic view of human society that was universal in the Middle Ages was gone, functional and organic theory had not yet appeared, and the new institutions had not as yet demonstrated their capacity to carry on without or in despite of theory. The common plea in the seventeenth century that no man is an island, that the bell tolls for thee and me, would not have been made so insistently if the facts had not appeared otherwise. Much has been made of post-Hobbesian attempts at taming the Leviathan of the unlimited nation-state, but the appeal of Hobbes himself was to a more profound fear, the fear of the unlimited individual—Buffe-Coate, Fox, Winstanley, and Anabaptists such as those of Münster.

Spinoza holds the individualist view of man on several counts besides that of his involvement in the thought of his time. His metaphysics is nominalist, at least in intent, so that "society" or "mankind," for instance, cannot for him be anything but collective nouns that point to numerous concrete individual relations.[84] Further, his ethics is essentially the ethics of an individual seeking salvation in a world which may not contain one intimate friend or fellow traveler, in which the community of saints or the city of God are only the thinnest of abstractions. The actual seeking of salvation, of autonomy, itself seems to alienate one from society and fellow man; the early part of the *Tractatus de Intellectus Emendatione* contains sober advice on how the hatred of the common man for philosophers may be averted. The unity of soul, the true individuality of the understanding man, sets him apart from those who are immersed in social values and communal ignorance. This is not a peculiarly philosophic isolation; Bunyan's pilgrim is just as alone.

There are meanings of "individualism" which Spinoza does not accept. Far from glorying, with the romantics, in the

[84] TTP, XVI, 125.

differences between men, he holds that nothing can be more alike than the ideas of two rational creatures; the nineteenth-century cult of personality would be, for him, mere confusion of mind. Economic individualism, particularly in the form of social Darwinism, would make even less sense to Spinoza, who thought that men needed to cooperate to the limit of their capacity if they were to achieve any good.

Man and Man

Spinoza bridges his psychology and his political thought with a doctrine of the relationship of man to man.

A man is aware of the existence of other men, as he knows of other objects, through his senses alone. His knowledge of them, according to Spinoza's epistemology, is therefore more imaginative than rational. Men are further separated from each other by the inherent faultiness of intersubjective communication. When such communication operates well, we commonly find in each other's minds more of passion than of reason—and it is the passions that divide men, reason that unites them.

We may assume from external signs that others think much as we do and the fact of our mutual interdependence is inescapable. Our sense of individual inadequacy to cope with the world can lead us, sometimes, to accept the safety of conformity to the thought and ways of others; sometimes it leads us to attempt to persuade others to accept our own personal outlook as definitive of reality.[85]

Men compete with and oppress other men from ambition; they struggle for scarce goods and by their struggle may increase the scarcity; they may even struggle for goods only because they are scarce. The confusion of desire is very great: Spinoza instances the man who praises a woman he loves and who yet would be dismayed if others believed him, that is, if

[85] TP, I, par. 5.

others loved her also.[86] As the conflict of passions within a man make him an enemy of himself, so, as "men are by nature subject to these passions . . . so men are by nature enemies" to each other.[87]

How, then, is society possible?[88] In two places Spinoza uses the phrase "social animal" as a definition of man. In the first instance[89] it is reported as a saying of the Schoolmen, in the second[90] it is mentioned as a definition which is generally accepted. Spinoza agrees that "it is hardly possible to maintain life and cultivate the mind without mutual help,"[91] and, "men are scarcely able to lead a solitary life." Elsewhere he says that "no isolated individual has enough power to defend himself and procure the necessities of life, they desire political society by nature,"[92] and, "it is before all things useful to men to associate their ways of life."[93] These statements rather support the theory that man is a social animal by circumstance than that he is so by instinct or by the elementary necessities of his nature. Spinoza does not completely agree with Aristotle that man is a creature who becomes truly a man only in a developed political organization. Spinoza certainly favored such organization as an aid to many men in their struggle to preserve themselves at all levels of need, but he just as certainly believed that a single man in a bad society can yet achieve, though with more difficulty, whatever is possible to man in any kind of political society. In another sense, Spinoza's statement that man is a social animal is equivalent to his saying that he is a political animal, for society cannot survive without political organization.[94]

[86] E, IV, prop. 58; see also TP, II, par. 14.
[87] TP, VIII, par. 12; E, IV, props. 32, 34; TP, II, par. 14.
[88] Another phase of this question will be discussed in the next chapter.
[89] TP, II, par. 15.
[90] E, IV, prop. 35.
[91] TP, II, par. 15; TTP, V, 93.
[92] TP, VI, par. 1.
[93] E, IV, App. 12 (and App. 9).
[94] TP, I, par. 3.

A man is truly a social animal, is in harmony with other men, insofar as he and they subject themselves to the rule of reason.[95] To be rational is to follow one's interests intelligently; nothing is more useful to other men than a man who does this.[96] Not only is the ascent to rationality noncompetitive, because it is a prize which all can win and which is the easier to win for having been won by others, but the rational man is urged at all levels of his being and understanding to assist others to be as he is. As a creature of passion he wants others to adopt his thought and way of life; for his preservation and advancement in wisdom it is to his interest to live safely in a community of rational creatures who will not obstruct and who possibly will help him; at his level of most complete personal integration he will feel a sense of community with others which will compel him, at the cost of any personal sacrifice, to work toward the advancement of his fellows.[97] Finally, without any further effort, but merely by being what he is, the rational man fills for others the role of the exemplar, the living image of what might be, for those who might not otherwise have realized their own possibilities.

And so, concludes Spinoza, as only rational men are really men, so only they are really political animals,[98] and only those men who have some degree of rationality are capable of any degree of social life at all.[99]

Equality. Spinoza does not treat of the topic of the equality or inequality of man at length in any one place. A discussion of his scattered remarks will, however, serve to lead us from his consideration of human nature to his political thought.

It is customary to limit discussions of human equality to considerations of worth, right, and power.

[95] TP, II, par. 21; E, IV, prop. 35.
[96] E, IV, prop. 35; E, IV, prop. 18.
[97] TdIE, p. 6; E, IV, prop. 18; E, IV, App. 9.
[98] Aristotle *Politics* 1280b; TTP, V, 103: "man without obedience or reason is inhuman."
[99] E, IV, prop. 35.

In a consistently naturalistic philosophy such as that of Spinoza, where praise and blame are out of place, there is no transcendent vantage point from which one man may be judged of greater worth than another, for value itself relates only to man's view of his interests. From the standpoint of some particular individual, for instance, some other man or men will seem to have more worth to the interests of that individual than do others. If his judgment is correct, there is, for him, an objective inequality of worth among other men. Similarly, it should be possible to consider men in the light of their utilitarian value to mankind and so arrive at a general standard for judging individuals. Spinoza does not do so in any systematic way.

Men have, of course, equal right to do that which they can, but since their powers are not equal, their actual right is also not equal. Spinoza's position is, not that might *should* make right, but that it *does*. This is an important point, for it is evident that his political thought centers about power, not about right. It is necessary to keep in mind, however, that his attitude toward power is that of the detached scientist; he has neither the enthusiasm for it displayed by Callicles or Thrasymachus nor the distaste for it shown by Lord Acton.[100]

The important difference between men, then, lies in the difference in their power, power defined as the capacity of each to act in his own interest. Because this capacity is in turn at least roughly equal to the power of the understanding, it might appear that Spinoza has evaded the issue of the power of man over man. He has not done so, for such power, insofar as it is physical or arises out of a pre-emption of social power, is hardly distinguishable, to the subjected party, from the ordinary blind forces of nature. Insofar as the subjecting power depends on rational appeal, it is no longer a case of the power of man over man, but of reason over passion.

[100] There is a hint, at TP, VII, par. 27, that *both* political power and political powerlessness are corrupting.

There is a radical inequality of man in another sense, however, and one which we should expect to follow from Spinoza's "aristocratic epistemology." [101] Although all men are born in equal bondage to the passions,[102] they are not, even at birth, equally likely to achieve rationality and their inequality increases as they mature. As C. D. Broad puts it:

within a given species to say that one member is 'better' than another, simply means that it has the characteristic powers of the species to a greater degree and that it performs the characteristic functions of the species more efficiently.[103]

Spinoza sees little justification for the social distinctions that divide men: "it is power and culture which mislead us"; [104] the apparent disparities in the abilities of, say, aristocrats and plebeians, is perhaps completely artificial. It seems never to occur to Spinoza, as it did to Plato, that the best political arrangements might involve rule by the most rational persons. On the contrary, in his constitutional proposals, monarchs and aristocrats are considered to be quite ordinary people with no claim to possess more understanding than their subjects. No special political function is assigned to those who are more rational. The most we can say, and this only in conjecture, is that the wiser man might serve the function, as Spinoza himself did in making his constitutional proposals, of a latter-day "hero-founder," [105] an exemplar of the political spirit. Even in this case, the power of the wiser man, if effective, is the power of communicated vision, rather than political power as ordinarily conceived. There is no connection between the talents necessary to practical statesmanship and the "power" of a

---

[101] "Aristocratic epistemology"—some epistemologies, such as Plato's, seem necessarily to involve human inequality, others, such as that of Rousseau, with its appeal to a conscience better left uncultivated, imply human equality.

[102] E, IV, prop. 68: "*if* men were born free." (Emphasis added.)

[103] Pp. 35, 45; see also TTP (Dover), III, 49; E, III, prop. 57.

[104] TP, VII, par. 27.

[105] See Chapter VI, below, on hero-founders.

philosopher; the immediately effective power of the many is greater than that of the wise man; individual power conveys no right to rule beyond the capacity to seize command; finally, men involved in public business cannot live the life of reason [106]—a philosopher king would soon become vulgarized.

There is a striking lack of sentiment, even a certain hardness, in Spinoza's view of the inequality of men:

For a horse is excuseable for being a horse and not a man; nevertheless it must be a horse and not a man. He who goes mad from the bite of a dog is, indeed, to be excused, and yet is rightly suffocated, and, lastly, he who is unable to control his desires, and to restrain them through fear of the laws, although he must be excused for his weakness, is nevertheless unable to enjoy peace of mind, and the knowledge and love of God, but necessarily perishes.[107]

At another place, he refers to Romans ix. 21: "Hath not the potter power over the clay, of the same lump to make one vessel unto honour, and another unto dishonour?" [108] The power of God, the way things are, is beyond criticism or demur. It is foolish to call this the best or worst of all possible worlds; it is the only possible world. The kingdom of God is not for children; the weak shall not be exalted; rather: " 'folly is the punishment of fools.' " [109] Those who call Spinoza a liberal are not entirely mistaken unless they confuse him with others similarly called who lack his stern commitment to realism.

Spinoza is clearly in favor of the legal equality of men as a practical political measure. When he says that "to demand equality between unequals is to demand the absurd," [110] he is

[106] TP, I, par. 5.
[107] Wolf, *Correspondence*, Ep. 78, p. 358; see also Ep. 21, p. 174.
[108] Wolf, *Correspondence*, Ep. 75, p. 347; see also TTP, p. 247, n. 34; TP, II, par. 22.
[109] TTP, IV, 85; also TTP, IV, 75.
[110] TP, IX, par. 4.

enunciating a general principle which applies to unequally powerful cities or nations. The individual is in quite a different case: "Citizens no doubt are rightly regarded as equal, since the power of an individual citizen is of no consequence when compared with the power of the state as a whole." [111] Equality of citizens contributes to the stability of the state; it is the equality of status in a democracy which most strongly recommends this form of government.[112] Yet even legal equality is not absolutely desirable as an end in itself; if political analysis indicates that an aristocracy is the most effective form of government in a given set of circumstances, Spinoza will opt for an aristocracy and retreat to the position that at least all aristocrats should be equal,[113] and even here not as a matter of abstract principle.

Groups, societies, and nations differ in strength and are therefore unequal in right. Do they also differ in rationality? Spinoza notes of the Jews that, in regard to "matters, wherein man's true happiness consist, they were on a par with the rest of the nations," [114] "there was no difference between Jew and Gentile"; [115] rationality is not a gift peculiar to any people; [116] "freedom or strength of mind is a private virtue; the virtue of a state is stability." [117] Nevertheless, although a society cannot itself achieve rationality, except in a metaphorical sense, different societies supply the conditions of rationality to their members to varying degrees.[118] Societies and constitutions are unequally useful, then, and therefore are unequal in human value.

[111] *Ibid.*
[112] TTP, XVII, 179; TTP, XVI, 137; Machiavelli, *Discourses*, I, ch. 55, p. 335.
[113] TP, X, par. 8.
[114] TTP (Dover), III, 48.
[115] TTP (Dover), III, 49.
[116] TTP, III, 55, 65.
[117] TP, I, par. 6.
[118] TTP, XVII, 181; TTP, III, 57.

The Exemplar and the Improvement of the Understanding
". . . as all who listen to philosophers become philosophers . . ." [119]

. . . man conceives a human character much more stable than his
own, and sees that there is no reason why he should not himself
acquire such a character. Thus he is led to seek for means which
will bring him to this pitch of perfection, and calls everything
which will serve as such means a true good. The chief good is that
he should arrive, together with other individuals if possible, at the
possession of the aforesaid character. What that character is we
shall show in due time, namely, that it is the knowledge of the
union existing between the mind and the whole of nature. [120]

A difficulty has been raised [121] about the availability to Spinoza, on the theoretical ground of its inconsistency with his
nominalism, of an "end of man" involving the concept of an
exemplar, a moral ideal. The objection seems not well
founded. The opening lines of the above passage make it plain
that Spinoza's exemplar bears no relationship either to an Aris-
totelian final cause exerting a positive attractive power or to a
Platonic ideal type. [122] My exemplar is my imaginative portrayal of myself as a more effective person, though it may take
the form of an idealization of an historical personage such as
Christ or Socrates. The only difference, in fact, between Spinoza's exemplar and Dewey's "end-in-view," both thoroughly
naturalistic, is to be found in Dewey's failure to relate human
ideals to a concept of human nature in relation to which it
would be significant to speak of one condition of man as

[119] TTP (Dover), p. 269, n. 2.
[120] TdIE, p. 6; see also TTP, XVI, 121; *Short Treatise,* p. 76; Knight, p.
379: "By virtue of the formal function of the superego man is able to take
himself as an object for reflection and evaluation. Through it, also, man has
the capacity to rise above himself, above his instinct, above his past, and
project himself into the future, to objectivise himself and conceive of
himself as different, better, happier, more successful."
[121] Bidney, p. 272; Martineau, *Types of Ethical Theory,* p. 372.
[122] Machiavelli, *The Prince,* Ch. VI, pp. 19–20.

better than another, and, following this failure, his conversion of ethics into sociology.[123]

An ethical system, for Spinoza, to repeat and expand a previous statement, is an explanation of the order of things, of man's nature and of its relationship to that order, an account sufficiently detailed to enable us in its light to arrive at a greater degree of pleasure, "self-preservation," and autonomy by way of the enlightenment of the passions. The vision of the exemplar is a vision not of an impossible perfection, but of a better position which can be reached.

Despite some substantial underlying metaphysical differences, Spinoza's concept of the exemplar as a critique of ordinary life, as the principle of innovation for the breaking of the vicious cycle in our lives of stale, compulsive, reactive repetitiousness, bears striking resemblance to older practices of the embodiment in particular persons of ethical or religious ideals. The differences are also worth noting. Spinoza's intent is not to posit a culture hero, an object of idle daydreams of limitless power, the ground of guilty self-reproach, or the excuse for lofty denunciation of human nature as it is ordinarily expressed in action. His concrete program includes, in the *Tractatus de Intellectus Emendatione* and in the *Ethics*, a method for the improvement of the understanding and enlightenment of the passions and, in the *Tractatus Theologico-Politicus* and *Tractatus Politicus*, a method for understanding and improving our social and political arrangements.

The *de Emendatione* is principally concerned with prelimi-

___

[123] No especial attack on Dewey is intended. I hope I do not go too far in assuming general agreement with the thought that modern ethical theory, insofar as it is not naturalistic, is not acceptable, and that insofar as it is not Spinozistic, it is not ethical. I take to be not naturalistic those systems which are based on natural law, authority, or intuition, not ethical those systems which describe how ethical decisions are or might be arrived at but which give us no metaphysical basis for choosing one decision over another— systems, that is, which do not purport to say what is good for man. I admit that this does not leave us many, if any, ethical systems to deal with. Is not just that the general complaint?

nary methodological arguments: epistemology, logic of thought, and the pursuit of the sciences for the bettering of man. The theme of the *Ethics* is the supersession of blind passion by knowledge, the "where there was id there shall be ego" program, the achievement of personal autonomy in the light of the steady order of the intellect.[124] In various places practical proposals are made in the form of programs for self help.[125] Finally:

Generally speaking, all legitimate objects of human desire fall under three heads: knowledge of things through their primary causes; control of the passions, or the formation of a virtuous disposition; security and physical health. The direct means to the first two goods, their proximate and efficient causes if you like, are contained in human nature itself; so that their attainment largely depends on our own unaided power, *i.e.*, on the laws of human nature alone. We must therefore insist that these gifts are not peculiar to any people, but have always been common to the whole human race; unless, perhaps, we are prepared to indulge in the dream that nature once created men of different species. But the means to security and physical survival lie mainly in things outside us. Accordingly, these goods are called gifts of fortune, because they are largely dependent on the unknown operation of external causes; so much so that in these matters a man's folly or prudence may make very little difference to his lot. Still, human guidance and vigilance can do a great deal to help men live in safety and avoid injury from other men and wild animals: and the surest means to this end, the means prescribed by reason and experience, is to form a society with definite laws, to occupy a particular stretch of territory, and to concentrate the strength of all the members in a single body, the body of the society. But to form and maintain a society requires ability and vigilance of no mean order. Hence a society formed and guided in the main by prudent and vigilant men will be more secure, more stable, and less at the mercy of fortune . . .[126]

[124] E, IV, prop. 66; E, IV, App. 4.
[125] E, IV, prop. 70; E, V, prop. 10; E, V, prop. 20; TTP, VII, 109.
[126] TTP, III, 55.

V

Man in Society

❖

THE application in the seventeenth century of the compositive-resolutive method of science to the fundamental questions of man's political organization may be seen to have produced some paradoxical conclusions. For example: given the premises that government without consent is not legitimate, that men are not bound to obey illegitimate government, that individual conscience is superior to all authority, and that men, or most men, even in their intellect and in what they call the promptings of conscience, are creatures of passion, it follows that no legitimate government can be had, for the voluntary adherence of many men for very long to any government is seen to be a practical impossibility.

On the other hand, of course, government is a necessity. What is necessary cannot be illegitimate. It follows that despotic government, since that is all that is possible, must be legitimate, and that if it is both legitimate and necessary, then it must also be desirable.

The difficulties at this point pushed the problem back to the more general question: Under what conditions, if any, is social order possible?

Before we consider Spinoza's search for a middle way between anarchy and despotism, a search in which he attempted to solve the problem of social order, it would be well to take account of those modern functional sociologists who seem to deny the reality of this problem.[1] Two lines are commonly taken. First, every going society has effective means for internalizing the norm of sociality in its members. Unsocial behavior is therefore characterizable as deviance caused by cultural deprivation or mental disorder. Second, man is an approval-seeking animal, dependent on the reception of a steady stream of information from others confirming his existence, his role, his worth.[2] Once again, unsocial behavior is to be understood simply as individual deviance, explicable in terms of ego disintegration or failure in social communication.

There is no point in denying the reality of these important socializing factors. In regard to the first, however, Freud himself did not believe that the superego played a major role in guiding the actions of most people. Further, the formulation ignores the conflict within the individual between socially implanted attitudes and perceived reality or personal interest, not to mention the social conflicts that arise between persons and groups with even slightly different standards of conscience. The second argument against the possibility of social conflict simply goes too far: the banker's desire for social approval does not lead him to approve all loan applications—if it did he would lose the approval of his board of directors. It is not necessary, in other words, that approval be given by all, that of a selected group will do. As between groups, approval may sometimes be sought, but often groups maintain their existence and inner solidarity only on the condition of external hostility. Both functionalist arguments, really, raise the question in a new form: How is social *disorder* possible? and answer it in terms of individual or societal insufficiency; no

---

[1] For much of both the statement of and the reply to the functionalist view, I am indebted to an article by Dennis Wrong, "The Oversocialized Conception of Man in Modern Society," pp. 183–92.

[2] *Ibid.*, p. 185, Wrong quotes Hans Zetterberg: "The maximization of favorable attitudes from others would thus be the counterpart in sociological theory of the maximization of profit in economic theory."

allowance is made for the possibility of conflict arising out of the social structure itself or out of inalterable exigencies of the human plight.

Of course Spinoza, along with most major political thinkers, recognizes the importance of socially induced attitudes to the stabilization of society.[3] He speaks often and at length of the social relevance of habit, awe, and conscience. As for the quest for approval:

In the case of fame [4] the mind is still more absorbed, for fame is conceived as always good for its own sake, and as the ultimate end to which all actions are directed . . . [it] has the further drawback that it compels its votaries to order their lives according to the opinions of their fellowmen, shunning what they usually shun, and seeking what they usually seek.[5]

The concept of a culturally conditioned conscience, and that of man as the seeker of approval, are both integral to Spinoza's political theory, but neither separately nor in conjunction are they thought to solve the problem of social conflict. Spinoza is here close to Machiavelli's position, that "man's inherent egoism means that conflict is the basic pattern of social behavior." [6] Machiavelli further distinguishes between the unlimited conflict arising out of personal egoism in a corrupt society and the ordered conflict that takes place within a framework of law, and between internal and external conflict, their reciprocal relationships, and the connection they have with forms of government. Spinoza's similar but more general treatment of these matters will be discussed in the next chapter.

[3] E, III, prop. 31; E, III, def. 27.
[4] The Latin is "fama," meaning "good opinion" as well as "fame."
[5] TdIE, p. 4; see also E, III, prop. 29.
[6] Wood, p. 51; also Machiavelli, *The Prince*, Ch. 18, p. 64; *Discourses*, I, Ch. 4, p. 219.

The State of Nature

Many political writers have made some use of the concept of a state of nature. If we ignore the few references which may be mere flights of fancy, the rest will be found to be a consideration either of what the state of man would be in the sudden absence of his political institutions, or the initial point of an imaginative or logical reconstruction of present institutions from a hypothetical prepolitical condition. A political philosophy which did not attempt to consider the life of man prior to the institution of the state might even be considered somewhat incomplete.

Spinoza has no interest in showing that the state of nature was actually exemplified in the past: [7] "all men, savage and civilized alike, everywhere enter into social relations and form some kind of civil order." [8] Neither does he find it necessary to assume therein a state of war of all against all:

Men who live in barbarous fashion without any political organization live, as we see, a miserable and almost brutish existence, and they cannot provide themselves with even the few commodities which they do possess, wretched and crude though these be, without mutual help of some sort or other.[9]

The form of any state of nature is given in the definition; the content is influenced, perhaps almost to the point of determination, by that view of society which is itself supposed to be the result of a particular state of nature. The important question, of course, is not whether we have seen the magician put the rabbit into the hat, it is whether it is a good rabbit. If a state of nature is to serve its purpose it must, without regard to its consequences, be convincing.

Hobbes's state of nature is horrible almost beyond description; even within civil society it is both imminent and imma-

[7] TP, II, par. 15; Pufendorf, II, 154.
[8] TP, I, par. 7; see also TP, I, par. 3; Wernham, p. 21.
[9] TTP, V, 93.

nent; any government is to be preferred to it, and no risk of bringing it back upon us is ever justified. Locke, who favored revolution under some circumstances, diminished accordingly both the terror of the state of nature and the danger of a return to it. Spinoza's description of the state of nature is fairly close to that of Hobbes in some important respects.[10] Yet he thought, as did Locke, that we could afford to exercise some discrimination in the matter of how we are to be governed and that, though with quite a different meaning of the word "right," the right of revolution could not be withheld from subjects.

Spinoza's use of the state of nature concept is paradigmatic, a link in the chain of his reasoning from the nature of things and of man to the civil state. The kind of interest man has in his government is best shown by contrasting his life under it with his life outside it:

Like sin and disobedience in the strict sense, justice and injustice are inconceivable except in a state. For there is nothing in nature which could rightly be said to belong to one man and not to another; all things belong to all, to all, that is, who have the power to appropriate them to themselves.[11]

. . . without mutual help men live in utter wretchedness, and are inevitably debarred from the cultivation of reason, we shall see very clearly that to live safely and well men had necessarily to join together.[12]

We have already seen that, except to the extent to which they are ruled by reason, men are naturally at odds with each other. They will therefore live in the condition of greatest mutual animosity in that state in which reason has the least force and where it is least likely to be developed: the state of nature.[13]

[10] TTP, XVI, 143, 145; TP, I, par. 23.
[11] TP, II, par. 23.
[12] TTP, XVI, 129; see also TTP, XIX, 207.
[13] TP, I, par. 5.

If we consider Spinoza only as the disciple of Hobbes or as an apostle of the Enlightenment, we should think he is now finished with the state of nature and about to produce the happy ending of the social contract. He is, however, more, and has yet more to say. There is a long tradition of friendly receptivity toward the idea of a state of nature, variously known also as the Garden of Eden, the Golden Age, "Arcady"—a tradition continued to this day by Rousseau, D. H. Lawrence, N. O. Brown, and others. The state of nature, that is to say, in spite of its being a situation of physical and cultural deprivation, has some compensatory attractions. Grant the fantasy of men living without government, in innocence and peace, in economic and intellectual simplicity, the social contract would be seen to initiate the reign of King Stork, the loss of political innocence, the invention of *amour propre* and of property.[14]

Of course not even Rousseau advocated the return to the woods. The sadness of adults does not lead them to envy children; our nostalgia for the freedom of polymorphous perverseness may be indulged by alcoholic reverie, by scholarly editions of De Sade, or by less pretentious editions of Bat Man, but we would not go back to it. Nor is this entirely because we are well trained, or merely afraid to live, or trapped in our artificially induced neuroses, or like the old dray horse turning back to the hard pavement from a sight of green fields, knowing that it is too late. The function of the state of nature in some political thought is to serve as an ideal point of departure in the syndrome of departure-and-return, but of return with a difference. For Augustine, for example, the journey of man is from the happiness of Eden to the happiness of Heaven by way of the earthly city—but Heaven is not Eden. Again, in the case of Rousseau's journey from the woods of the *Origins of Inequality* to the village of the *Social*

---

[14] It is odd that Augustine's band of robbers, the State, should invent property. Was Proudhon right and Kant naive?

Contract, the route is by way of the slavery of the city. The goal must contain the beginning, however transformed; the paradox offered is that man is without a home, that he cannot go home again, but that he need not be homeless.[15]

And so, for the interim, there is the appeal of Hobbes, who tells us not to be fools but to face the facts, to shelve our libertarian fantasies and swallow the bitter pill of the unlimited state. We face his facts, not wanting to be fools, even happy ones, if that were possible. And so also, for the longer run, it is the appeal of Spinoza, and Rousseau, that they knew that not all who cry "facts! facts!" shall see the truth, that they faced Hobbes's facts and went on to use them for human ends. The state of the hero founder makes an excellent drill-field for the forming of social men; the state of Hobbes is a reasonable hospital for a nation battered by a generation of disorder. Yet, although men may on occasion need drill-fields and hospitals, these are not homes for the human spirit.

Spinoza and Rousseau each refer to the necessity for retaining elements of the state of nature in a reasonable society, Rousseau in his "and each remains as free as before," Spinoza at various places, where he says that democracy is closest to the state of nature and therefore most desirable, and where the best government is defined as that which is felt not to govern at all. It is not felt to govern because its commands have been completely internalized, accepted. Propaganda cannot accomplish this complete coincidence of public and private judgment.[16]

The state of nature, then, plays a double part in Spinoza's thought; it is at once the condition of bestiality out of which we have arisen and the community of saints which lies just over the horizon of his political doctrine.

[15] Brown, p. 84: "Mankind is that species of animal which has the immortal project of recovering its own childhood. But childhood is the state of nature. The notion of man's revolt from nature and return to nature . . ."

[16] TTP (Dover), III, 53.

Spinoza's practical, and central, problem is the finding of a middle way between the original state of nature and despotism. We have seen that he does not completely reject the state of nature. What of despotism? As we shall see in the next chapter, he does not completely reject despotism either, but sees it as a necessary, and therefore desirable, stage of political development. A way out of the state of nature is through the despotism of the hero founder.

The Social Contract

Apparently only in periods such as the seventeenth century, when radical individualism was taken for granted, when actual conflict between the individual and the state was common, and when the proper relationship between sovereign and subject was generally disputed, does it seem necessary to arrive at a theory of the obligation of the citizen to obey the law which is based on the legal fiction of a contract, a contract not merely to live under a particular government, but to live in society at all.[17]

In speaking as he does of the social contract, then, Spinoza is a man of his time, yet we should note the special treatment he accords it. He does not believe, first, that it ever happened—the covenant of the Jewish people with God, or with Moses, is clearly understood to be a myth—or, second, that it entails any obligation to obey. The social contract for Spinoza is merely an explanatory device to make clear some fundamental and necessary relations between men in civil society; it has no reference to possible or actual historical events; it is a purely rational exercise in human relations:

Since men, as I said, are led more by passion than by reason, their natural motive for uniting and being guided as by one mind is not reason, but some common passion; common hope, or common fear, or a common desire to avenge some common injury.[18]

---

[17] d'Entreves, *Natural Law*, p. 55.
[18] TP, VI, par. 1; see also TP, I, par. 5.

The rational argument is:

To create a state the one thing needful was that all power to make decisions should be vested either in all collectively, or in a few, or in one man; for the great diversity of men's free judgements, the claim of each to have a monopoly of wisdom, and their inability to think alike and speak with one voice made it impossible for men to live at peace unless everyone surrendered his right to act entirely as he pleased.[19]

The last two lines require explication. Spinoza's general theory of natural right holds that man *never* surrenders his right to act as he pleases; how, then, can men ever live at peace with each other? The general explanation is that:

man acts in accordance with the laws of his own nature and pursues his own advantage in both the natural and the political order. In both conditions, I say, man is led by hope or fear either to do or to refrain from doing one thing or another. The chief difference between the two is that in the political order all fear the same things, and all have one and the same source of security, one and the same mode of life; but this, of course, does not deprive the individual of his power of judgement. For the man who decides to obey all the commands of the commonwealth, whether through fear of its power, or because he loves tranquility, is certainly pursuing his own security and advantage in accordance with his own judgement.[20]

This is to say that in entering the social contract the individual retains his right to do anything he pleases, but (and here the matter of the voluntary character of his entrance is shown to be irrelevant, or no longer relevant)[21] he finds the conditions under which that right may be asserted vastly changed. Some rights, that is to say powers, which he had in the state of

---

[19] TTP, XX, 231; see also TTP, V, 93; TTP, XVI, 133-37.
[20] TP, III, par. 3.
[21] "Surrender" may imply more of a contractual-obligational sense than Spinoza intended. Elwes (Dover, p. 259) translates "*cederet*" as "abdicated."

nature he now has no longer—they have been denied to him by the superior power of the state; some weaknesses or dangers to which he was subject in the state of nature are now absent. If he decides to obey the commands of the state he does so, not because he has promised to do so, but because he is afraid to disobey or because he finds his advantage in obeying.

To restate this in a more extended manner: Men in the state of nature are in a state of insecurity with regard to one another, are impoverished because of the necessarily primitive character of the means of production and the impossibility of capital formation, and have no hope of improving their condition in either respect. Further, in the ideal case, men would be so unenlightened as not to be aware of the possibility of improvement of either their physical or rational potentialities. Yet, if men could pool their forces, if an organization could be formed which would utilize the strength of all to protect each from violence and to guarantee property and contracts,[22] then, for as long as a sufficiently powerful fraction of the membership supported the organization, all would be compelled to obey it.

The following observations may be made on the above reasoning:

Before, during, and after the making of the contract, and whether one is subject to it by conquest, birth, or voluntary adherence, everyone has complete right to do anything which he can do. The conditions under which men determine what they wish to do have, of course, changed with the social

[22] TTP, III, 57: "the purpose of every state is secure and comfortable living." Spinoza does not equate a rise in the standard of living, or even in the level of culture, with that genuine advance which is toward rationality. At TP, X, par. 4, he speaks as a Machiavellian: "The fact is that in time of peace men lay aside their fear; savages and barbarians gradually become civilized and cultured, and culture in turn gives rise to softness and laziness; men no longer strive to surpass one another in courage, but in pride and extravagance; they thus begin to disdain the ways of their ancestors, to adopt foreign customs, in a word, to be slaves." See also TTP, III, 65. There is no reconciliation attempted in his text between Spinoza's epicureanism and his ideal of civic virtue—perhaps none is needed.

contract; they must reckon less on the danger from other men, from wild beasts and starvation, more on the danger of breaking the law. Men are now better enabled to make more far-seeing reckonings of their interests.

That newly created entity, the sovereign power, has the same right to do all that is in its power which any natural being enjoys.[23] For as long as it maintains its power to command, its subjects must obey it "in so far as they fear its power or its threats, or in so far as they love the political order." [24] The right of the subject against the sovereign, in turn, equals his own power against it, a power which must usually be very slight. There can be no question of a legal right against the sovereign,[25] except such as the sovereign itself chooses to concede, because the subject can either enforce such a right or he cannot. If he cannot, then he is completely subject to the superior power of the sovereign; if he can, then he is stronger than the sovereign and he, not it, is the sovereign.[26]

To the extent to which the sovereign may lose its power to enforce its commands, it also loses its right to command.[27] A return to the state of nature, however, does not follow. A new state, a new sovereign, will replace the old; men

desire political society by nature, and can never dissolve it entirely.

Thus the quarrels and rebellions which often arise in a commonwealth never lead the citizens to dissolve the commonwealth (as often happens in other kinds of association); if their quarrels cannot be composed otherwise, they simply change its form. Hence by the means required to preserve a state I understand those which are necessary to preserve its form without any notable change.[28]

---

[23] TP, III, par. 2.
[24] TP, III, par. 8.
[25] TP, IV, pars. 4, 5; TP, II, par. 21.
[26] TP, III, par. 3.
[27] TTP, XVI, 133, 135, 137.
[28] TP, VI, pars. 1, 2.

Does this mean that the contract has lapsed and must be renewed by a new sovereign with the people? This would be too literal an interpretation of what Spinoza meant by a social contract. In the course of a later discussion, below, it will be shown that Spinoza is best understood to mean by "social contract" the constant will of a society that there be a sovereign. The question of the origin of society itself, which emerges more insistently as the notion of a social contract retreats into ideality, will also have to be deferred, though for now it can be said that the original institution of the sovereign power would entail the coming into being of complex patterns of social attitudes, interdependencies, mores, habits, and expectations which would form a powerful inertial force against a relapse into the state of nature.

Although the effective right or power of the individual subject against the sovereign may be very slight, it does not follow that the power of the state against its members is unlimited.[29] Because the power of the state consists solely in the collected strength of its subjects, that power is limited not only by the extent of that strength but also by the efficiency of the state mechanism in utilizing it and the actual degree of adherence and support given by the subjects. Further, just as I do not have the power to compel my desk to eat grass, so the power of the state does not extend to the capacity to compel its subjects to do those things which violate the laws of human nature: to hate their friends or to believe what is incredible.[30] Again, if the state alienates the affections of many of its subjects, it may find the remainder insufficient to uphold its power.[31] Finally, the maximum support can only be had

[29] TTP, XVII, 153.
[30] TP, III, par. 8.
[31] As an exercise in pure theory, Spinoza questions the "right" of the state to do that which weakens it. As a man may be said to have no right to do that which weakens him, because right is power and power is capacity to preserve oneself, so self-debilitation is weakness, the opposite of right. TP, III, par. 9; TP, IV, par. 4.

when the subject offers it voluntarily. Such voluntary support can be had only in return for real benefits.[32]

It is noteworthy that, without any recourse to traditional notions of a natural law limiting the actions of sovereigns, or of a natural moral right of subjects, without reference to national character or history, to contract or to constitutions, but purely by an analysis of the nature of political power, Spinoza has gone far toward the taming of the Leviathan.

As has been said, the move out of the state of nature [33] and the actual character of the power relationships which ensue between subjects and sovereign, are entirely theoretical constructions and may not be reflected in the subjective apprehension of any, and certainly not of most, of the subjects or of the sovereign itself.[34] Those reasons which are adequate for an action are not necessarily those motivating the agents of the action. Further, both subjects and sovereigns, under the influence of self-serving imagination, are likely to believe they have rights beyond their actual power to enforce. Such beliefs, for Spinoza, are in the realm of political pathology.

Society and the State

Spinoza distinguishes, but does not separate, society from the state. Ideally,

if human nature were such that men desired nothing but what true reason prescribes, a society would admittedly need no laws whatsoever; for men to do of their own free will what is really for their benefit it would be quite enough to teach them true moral precepts.[35]

Since this is not the case, "no society can exist without government and force, and hence without laws to control and restrain the unruly appetites and impulses of men." [36]

[32] TTP, V, 95; TTP, XVI, 135; TTP, XVII, 151; TP, VII, par. 11.
[33] TP, III, par. 6.
[34] TP, I, par. 7.
[35] TTP, V, 93.
[36] Ibid.

Spinoza's concept of the relationship between state and society is distinct from that held either by Hobbes or by Locke; it is closest, perhaps to the view of Machiavelli. It was necessary to Hobbes's argument for the Leviathan that society not be separable from the state, that no intermediate social organization exist to blur the sharp distinction between state of nature and civil society. For Locke, on the contrary, human society seems to be eternal and pervasive; it exists in the state of nature, it ratifies the social contract, it sits in permanent court over every constitution or regime which comes into being. Given a minimum of original social organization, Spinoza's view of an interaction between society and state has some advantages. He sees a hero-founder, the state personified, forming the character of a society; later the character of the society determines the form of the government. Between these extremes of dominance, society and state reciprocally determine each other—as we shall now proceed to show.

VI

Subjects and Hero-Founders

❖

Subjects

IF Spinoza's belief that political knowledge can and should be deduced from knowledge of human nature is correct, the preceding generalities about that nature should have given us some intimation of what to expect of actual peoples in concrete historical situations. His view of society is that, in an ordinary community, we will find: a few men, so completely subject to impulse, so unaware of their long-range, true interests, that only the unintermittent use or threat of force can restrain them from breaking the peace; yet fewer men, so subject to the rule of reason, so well aware of their interests, that no force at all is required to insure their obedience to law (any but the most irrational regimes may count on their active support);[1] a great number of men who fall between the above two categories.[2] The study of politics is mainly concerned with this group; they are "the people," they include all who are neither above the need for the state, as are gods and rational men,[3] nor below the level of political life, as are beasts or delinquents.

Of the people we may say that they are ruled, both politically and in their personal lives, by a mixture of reason and passion. More precisely, they are ruled by opinion, which is to say, by the custom of the community, by awe (*aidos*) or

[1] TTP, V, 93; TTP, XVI, 131; TP, III, par. 6.
[2] TTP, IV, 69; TTP, XVII, 153.
[3] Wolf, *Correspondence*, Ep. 19, p. 150.

myth, by habit, by personal interest conventionally understood, and by ignorance, the inadequate structuring of incomplete experience.[4]

A man of the people may refrain from stealing because he
knows it to be against his best interests, because "honesty is
the best policy," because it violates a supernatural injunction,
because he feels it to be wrong, because others will disapprove
of him if he steals, because he will be punished if caught, or
because he is not in the habit of getting things that way. Each
of these deterring considerations is interesting on its own account; for the moment we must consider the matter of their
sheer number.[5]

The area between total rationality and total incorrigibility
is vast and populous. The people are not an homogeneous
group, even at one time and place; the rational development of
each individual is both uneven and unstable.[6] Therefore, between the extremes of rational appeal and capital punishment,
society has evolved a whole arsenal of motivations to social
behavior to match the variety of temperaments and moods of
a people and of each member of it.[7] Sole reliance on punitive
measures is not enough, as the history of capital punishment is
supposed to show, and in any case sufficient force is seldom if
ever available to cope with a whole nation or even with all the
occasions of one man. The principle of the economy of means
dictates the use of a wide spectrum of social pressures, operating both within and externally to the individual.[8]

The sum of the habits and opinions, the fears and expectations, of a people constitutes the national character. How this
character is formed will be discussed later; for the present we
can say of it that:

[4] TP, IV, par. 4; TP, VII, par. 12; TTP (Dover), Pref., 5; Machiavelli,
Discourses, I, Ch. 11, p. 242.
[5] TTP, XVII, 151; TTP, XIV, 113.
[6] TTP, V, 91.
[7] TTP, IV, 69.
[8] TTP, V, 95; TTP, XVII, 151.

Once established, it has great inertial force and can be studied as a natural phenomenon. The successful statesman must be presumed to understand it better than does the philosopher; its complexity is such as to call for intuitive rather than analytic powers, for art more than for science.[9] Because a people cannot be ruled either by reason or by force alone, it must be ruled also by the empirical art of humbuggery. The practical statesman knows what proportion of flattery and threat works best in what circumstances, how much of the veneer of rational appeal is effective, what must be ignored, what gods must be propitiated. Plato noted that a philosopher would be out of place in a political contest; Spinoza went on to the position that "no men are regarded as less fit to govern a state than theorists or philosophers." [10]

The habits of mind of a people dictate some and preclude other political arrangements. A people with a democratic tradition can be ruled by a king only with the greatest difficulty; a people accustomed to despotic rule are incapacitated for self-rule.[11] Communities differ among themselves in the degree of rationality achieved and therefore also in the degree of rationality they will tolerate or demand from their government.[12]

What does it mean to speak of the degree of "rationality" of a people? This is a good place to remind the reader of the necessity, in reading Spinoza, of remembering the special meanings he has given to his words. Rationality, it will be recalled, is a power, a power to arrive at useful goals by appropriate means. Rationality as a national characteristic is less likely to be manifested as a general capacity for formal logical thought than by success in war over a long period of time, a high standard of living, and the continuance of a stable

[9] TP, I, par. 2.
[10] TP, I, par. 1.
[11] TTP, V, 95; Machiavelli, *The Prince,* Ch. V, pp. 18–19.
[12] TP, X, par. 9.

and unrepressive form of government.[13] To be rational, for a nation or for a person, is to be realistic, or, in order to avoid some invidious connotations of that word, we might say that it is an orientation toward fidelity to the reality principle.[14]

Individually, "citizens are not born but made,"[15] they are made by the national character to which they are born and which they transmit. Each citizen, then, is socially plastic; the society itself is relatively rigid. Where does society come from?

Hero-Founders

Political theorists employing the concepts "state of nature" and "social contract" will commonly encounter difficulties in explaining the actual transition from the first to the second. Spinoza does not insist on the historical factuality of a state of nature in the pure sense—there is always some degree of communality—and he sees the social contract, insofar as it is more than a methodological scaffolding, as a product of passion rather than of calculation.[16] On the other hand, his principle that men are least rational in the state of nature, and therefore in a condition of maximum mutual animosity, creates for him the problem of how the national character could come into being.

Spinoza adopts the classical, and Machiavellian,[17] concept of the hero-founder. It must be admitted that he does not formally advance this device as a general principle of explanation, yet his only account of the formation of a national character consists of a detailed application of the hero-founder thesis to a Biblical narrative. Later, and more generally, he says:

[13] TTP, III, 57; TTP (Dover), II, 48; TTP, IV, 85.
[14] TP, II, par. 8.
[15] TP, V, par. 2.
[16] TP, VI, par. 1.
[17] Machiavelli, *The Prince*, Ch. VI, p. 21; *Discourses*, I, Ch. 2, p. 211; I, Ch. 9, pp. 233–36; I, Ch. 17, p. 257.

Human nature is such that men cannot live without some common system of law. Now such systems have been established, and public affairs conducted, by men of great acuteness—call them astute or cunning as you please . . .[18]

The long history now assigned to mankind, the decline of great-man theories of history, and the present functional view of society, seem to have combined to relegate hero-founder theories to the realm of the quaint unless, that is, we have merely substituted one phrase for another, "charismatic leader" for "hero-founder." The function of the concept in either form is to account for institutional innovation.[19] Spinoza is not induced to use the hero-founder theory for lack of sufficient historical time to account for man's social development;[20] his universe is not created but has existed from eternity, and although his writings contain no hint of a theory of how man came to be, it is clear that Spinoza did not believe that he was created. Further, unlike Machiavelli or Rousseau, Spinoza never considers the hero-founder as a possible reformer of existing society; his only function is the creation of the national character.[21]

Let us follow Spinoza in his explanation of the founding of the Jewish state by Moses.[22]

The account falls into two parts: the initial grasp of power and the formation of a people.

At the beginning of the story, the Jews were in the state of nature:

once they had been freed from the intolerable yoke of the Egyptians and were not bound by pact to any mortal man, they

[18] TP, I, par. 3.

[19] It is not intended that all differences between the two phrases are to be denied, yet the parallel between Spinoza's account of the hero-founder Moses and the description of charismatic leadership given by Weber is striking. See: *From Max Weber: Essays in Sociology*, pp. 294–98.

[20] Wolf, *Correspondence*, Ep. 4, p. 83.

[21] Rousseau, *Social Contract*, Bk. II, Ch. 7, pp. 37–42.

[22] TTP (Dover), VII, 105: "Moses . . . strove to found a well-ordered commonwealth."

regained their natural right to do everything in their power; and each could decide afresh whether he would retain it or surrender and transfer it to another.[23]

They were not, it is true, in the state of elementary savagery of those who have had no experience of society, but they were not capable of forming a state by themselves:

As soon as the Jews left Egypt they were no longer bound by the laws of any other people, and were thus free to establish new laws or make new ordinances as they pleased, to maintain a state wherever they wished, and to occupy any lands they desired. Yet they were utterly incapable of framing laws wisely and of holding sovereignty collectively; for none of them had much experience and they were worn out by the miseries of slavery.[24]

All that was left to them was a trusted leader, Moses, and their faith in God: "Having thus reverted to the condition of nature, they took the advice of Moses, in whom they had the greatest confidence, and decided to transfer their rights to no mortal man, but to God alone." [25] God does not function as an earthly sovereign, of course, as Moses must have known, and "in fact the Jews retained their sovereignty completely." "The covenant left them all completely equal, and all had an equal right to consult God and to receive and interpret his laws; in short, they were all equally in charge of the whole administration of the state." [26] Note that Spinoza is not describing democracy here, or "holding sovereignty collectively," but anarchy. Although there was as yet no Jewish state to contain the church-state problem or to which the individual conscience could oppose itself, this is a statement of one of the most serious of seventeenth-century political problems in brief. An ironic note appears when, the story contin-

[23] TTP, XVII, 157; TTP (Dover), II, 38–39.
[24] TTP, V, 95–97.
[25] TTP, XVII, 157; TTP, XVIII, 191, where it is said that such a covenant is no longer possible.
[26] TTP, XVII, 159.

ues, the people go to speak with God, their new sovereign: "But at this first approach they were so terrified and thunder-struck at hearing God speak that they thought their last hour was at hand." [27] In utter panic they returned to Moses,

saying, 'Behold we have heard God speaking in the fire, and why should we wish to die? . . . Go thou nigh therefore, and hear all the words of our God; and thou (not God) shalt speak unto us. Every command God shall give to thee we shall obediently per-form.' By these words they obviously abolished the original cove-nant, transferring their right to consult God and to interpret his decrees to Moses without reserve.[28]

Call Moses "astute or cunning, as you please," [29] Spinoza makes it clear that the roundabout route to power was the most effective. If Moses had initially offered himself as a sovereign, his power would have been much less than it was now that he had interposed himself between God and the people.[30]

For the ordinary statesman, gaining and keeping control depends only on his ability to play on existing mass emotions and prejudice.[31] The hero-founder has the incomparably greater task of the creation of a predictable pattern of such reactions out of a chaos of individual passions, of the creation, that is, of the national character. Our own century furnishes more examples of the techniques necessary to accomplish these ends than Spinoza could have known, but his formula-

[27] *Ibid.*

[28] TTP, XVII, 161; Deut. 5:24–27; Machiavelli, *Discourses*, I, Ch. 11, pp. 241–42.

[29] TP, I, par. 3; TTP (Dover), VII, 102–103; Spinoza's opinion of Moses as a representative of God appears a few pages before, at TTP, XVII, 155–57, where the ancient practice of the deification of rulers is shown to be politically motivated. As contrasted with the Jews, "the Macedonians were too sensible" to be imposed upon so.

[30] TTP, XVII, 161–63; TTP, XIX, 209: "From then on Moses was an absolute monarch."

[31] TTP, V, 95.

tion seems adequate: a national religion or ideology,[32] internal terror, external war [33]—and out of this heat and smoke, the forging of a national character.

Once the spirit of resistance is broken, gentler means are found to be more efficient.[34] Spinoza sees the measures employed by Moses in forming the Jewish nation as dictated by universal political necessities.

Once Moses had assumed command as the official spokesman of God, the initial fear of the people subsided and

many of them, and these by no means commoners, became dissatisfied with this election, and so began to believe that Moses was doing nothing by divine decree, but was settling everything to suit his own pleasure . . . They therefore raised an uproar . . .

And Moses found no means of pacifying them; but a miracle was performed to distinguish the faithful, and they were all wiped out. This gave rise to a new and general revolt of the whole people, for it thought that the men had not been destroyed by God's judgement, but by a trick on Moses's part; and although Moses restored peace eventually after it had been exhausted by a great disaster or plague, it was in such straits that everyone thought death more welcome than life. Thus of that time it would be truer to say that rebellion had ceased than that harmony had been established.[35]

The statement that the initial revolt had been begun by those who were "by no means commoners," suggests an aristocratic uprising against the monarchical power of Moses. The most important lines, however, are at the end, where it is suggested that the people have become so abject and disorganized that they are ready for the impress of a new character, a new

[32] TTP, XVII, 177: "Hence the patriotism of the Jews was not only patriotism but piety."

[33] See Sorel, pp. 84–91, for the thesis that external violence promotes internal unity.

[34] TTP, V, 95: "As long as men act from fear alone, they act most unwillingly."

[35] TTP, XVII, 185–87.

national character. This is a critical part of the hero-founder concept. All institutions that require a degree of personal loyalty from members evolve "hazing" practices that involve a degree of ego-destruction, reorientation, and reconstitution of personality.[36] The substitution of one cultural ethos for another requires a more drastic application of the same measures.[37]

Moses's next step was the institution of what appear to be religious rules and rituals, but which in fact constitute a system of national "basic training":

Finally, to ensure that the people, which could not be its own master, should hang on the lips of its ruler, he did not allow his subjects—who were, of course, accustomed to slavery—to do anything at their own good pleasure; they could do nothing without having at once to recall the law and carry out instructions which depended wholly on the will of their ruler. They were not allowed to plough, sow, or reap as they pleased, but had to follow a fixed and definite legal prescription; similarly, they could not eat, dress, shave their heads or beards, make merry, or do anything whatsoever, except as the law instructed and pre-

[36] The institutions that come to mind are: colleges, military organizations, prisons, monasteries. Traces of such practices are found in almost every situation where a person newly arrived in a group is expected to behave modestly—an almost subliminal humiliation rite is here looked for. There are, of course, elements of a "reign of terror" even in the original acculturation process known as child training.

[37] The measures must be more drastic because they affect the whole outlook rather than one special phase of it. It is for this reason that no hero-founder can leave the family organization alone. The family is the principal "processor of new recruits" to society; if the family training is not reoriented, the new society cannot endure. Luke 14:26; Rousseau, *Social Contract*, p. 38: "He who dares to undertake the making of a people's institutions ought to feel himself capable, so to speak, of changing human nature, of transforming each individual, who is by himself a complete and solitary whole, into part of a greater whole from which he in a manner receives his life and being; of altering man's constitution for the purpose of strengthening it; and of substituting a partial and moral existence for the physical and independent existence nature has conferred on us all. He must, in a word, take away from man his own resources and give him instead new ones alien to him, and incapable of being made use of without the help of other men. The more completely these natural resources are annihilated, the greater and more lasting are those which he acquires . . ."

scribed. What is more, they were even required to have on their doorposts, hands, and foreheads certain signs to recall them continuously to obedience. Thus the object of sacred rites was that men should never act of their own volition, but always by the command of another, and should continually acknowledge by their thoughts and deeds that they were not their own masters but completely under another's control.[38]

In short, their life was a continual practice of obedience . . . so that obedience became second nature, and must have seemed to them no longer servitude but freedom.[39]

Throughout this difficult process, Moses had also to maintain his own power. Continual demonstration had to be made both of the power of God and of the fact that Moses was his sole authorized representative.[40] Such demonstrations took the form of actual successes in war and in internal struggles, displays of supernatural power, and actual advancement of the interests of the nation. When Spinoza speaks of the "divine power" which Moses had, he is referring to the natural power which produced success.[41] As for miracles, in view of Spinoza's rejection of them elsewhere, we must assume that he is, tongue in cheek, following Machiavelli's advice that the ruler of a superstitious people should produce whatever miracles are helpful.[42]

And so the Jewish nation is brought into being—complete with a peculiar way of life which stressed their difference from other peoples, and a justifying ideology.[43] It is clear that,

---

[38] TTP, V, 97–99. Compare with Plato's similar prescription at *Laws* 942, with Rousseau, *Emile*, p. 83, and with Machiavelli, *Discourses*, III, Ch. 36, p. 563.

[39] TTP, XVII, 179. The word "seemed" is important. Actually, TTP (Dover), II, 39: "The rule of right living . . . was to them rather a bondage than the true liberty."

[40] TTP, XIV, 113.

[41] TTP (Dover), I, 24–25; TTP (Dover), III, 45.

[42] Machiavelli, *The Prince*, Ch. XXVI, p. 96; *Discourses*, I, Ch. 11, pp. 241–42; TTP (Dover), VII, 102–103.

[43] TTP, XVII, 175–79; Coser, p. 153: "Groups which are engaged in continued struggle tend to lay claim on the total personality involvement of their members"; Rousseau, *Social Contract*, Bk. II, Ch. 7, p. 41.

despite his irony at the expense of Moses's supernatural pretensions and the simplicity of the Jewish people, Spinoza is far from condemning the hero-founder stage of history; it is a necessary part of the advance to better things. His own predilection is for a society marked by rationality and freedom, but he recognizes that good societies do not spring up like mushrooms, that omelets are not made without breaking eggs. (Ordinary despots break many eggs, but produce no omelets.) Neither does he regard Moses as a mere adventurer: he notes with approval the latter's decision not to hand down his power intact but to divide it [44] in such a way as to preserve the new institutions in an effective constitutional framework.

A study of Spinoza's extensive treatment of the career of Moses and of the political institutions of the Jews reveals a complex pattern of intentions.

Of some interest is the recurring theme of the origins of society and of the state. Sometimes this is taken as the abstract problem of the transition from the state of nature to the civil order and Spinoza offers both a rational social contract theory and a theory that society is formed by a sudden concurrence of the passions of men. At other times he sees the question to be of the origin of particular historical institutional patterns. Here again two theories are offered, one of the hero-founder and another of the workings of "chance" and adaptation over a long period of time. It seems quite possible to consider these suggestions as complementary rather than as conflicting hypotheses.

We may also see in Spinoza's account of the conflicts within Jewish society a mirror image of similar conflicts in the Netherlands, and we may read his comments on Jewish history

[44] TTP, XVII, 163–69; TTP, XIX, 217; Machiavelli, *Discourses*, I, Ch. 9, p. 234: "Furthermore, though but one person suffices for the purpose of organization, what he has organized will not last long if it continues to rest on the shoulders of one man, but may well last if many remain in charge and many look to its maintenance."

as a series of only slightly camouflaged comments on contemporary Dutch political troubles. He also uses Jewish history to illustrate his own political notions.

Meanwhile, Spinoza follows the standard practice of his own time in using the authority of the Bible to support his political ideas and to attack those of his opponents. This was, even then, a tired old game but one which every political thinker was obliged to play. At the same time, Spinoza is telling us that the Bible is not, on the basis of its own testimony, a good guide to political practice, for the civil constitution of the Jews did not work even for them. Naturally so, for it was inflicted on them by God as a punishment for their sins. Further, even if it had worked well for the Jews, this constitution is unsuited to the very different circumstances and character of the Dutch. The critical point here is that theocracy is incompatible with the prosperity of a trading nation.

Finally, we are told that the Bible has no present authority in political matters; its historical function was to teach obedience to a Jewish state which no longer exists.

Spinoza's acceptance of many of Machiavelli's political categories is clearest in his acceptance of the latter's hero-founder thesis. Machiavelli's hero-founder is not, of course, merely an idealized tyrant, but is the product partly of some very selective historical research, partly of ingenious psychological analysis, and partly of Machiavelli's own political ideals. If a prince is ambitious and seeks power and glory with extreme earnestness, then, if he is also intelligent and capable and sees the opportunity, he will be satisfied with nothing less than the creation of a new nation. This new nation, if it is to be a suitable and lasting monument to his fame, must contain automatic inner mechanisms to guarantee its future power and stability—that is to say, it must be a republic. And so, hedged by the necessities of political reality and lured on by an ambition which is wholly self-regarding, the hero-founder is "trapped" into the performance of the most virtuous deed possible, the founding of a republic of free and virtuous men. If Spinoza is a Machiavellian in his hero-founder theory, Machiavelli must be seen as a Spinozist in his power theory: power, rightly understood, can be a force only for good.[45]

[45] Augustine *City of God* v. 12, 18; Machiavelli, *Discourses,* I, Ch. 10, pp. 236–39; II, Ch. 2, pp. 365–66.

VII

Constitutional Proposals

❖

SPINOZA'S *Tractatus Politicus*, never completed, is the only work of his which is solely, or even principally, devoted to political matters. Almost three-fourths of the book consists of the presentation of model constitutions: [1] a monarchy, an aristocracy, and a democracy.

The first chapter opens with a contrast between the political writings of philosophers and of statesmen. Philosophers have failed to consider human nature as it is, thinks Spinoza, and so they "have never conceived a political system which can be applied in practice; but have produced . . . obvious fantasies," and, "No men are regarded as less fit to govern a state than theorists or philosophers." [2] "Statesmen, on the other hand, are believed to plan men's undoing rather than their welfare, and have a greater reputation for cunning than for wisdom." "Yet there is no doubt that statesmen have written much more successfully about politics than philosophers; for since experience has been their guide, they have taught nothing which could not be put into practice." [3]

It is Spinoza's design to combine theory and practice, elimi-

[1] The Dover edition contains 29 pages (Chapters I through V) of general introduction, 29 pages on monarchy (Chapters VI and VII), 40 pages on aristocracy (Chapters VIII, IX, and X), and 3 pages on democracy (incompleted Chapter XI).

[2] TP, I, par. 1; Aristotle *Politics* 1288b: "Most of the writers who treat of politics . . . fail when they come to matters of practical utility"; Polybius *Histories* xii: 27; per contra, TTP, III, 55.

[3] TP, I, par. 2.

nating from the former its tendency toward fantasies arising out of false ideas of human nature, and from the latter its tendency to make of political studies a plot against the welfare of men. He asserts that every form of commonwealth has already been brought into existence at some time,[4] and thus,

> my object in applying my mind to politics is not to make any new or unheard of suggestions but to establish by sound and conclusive reasoning, and to deduce from the real nature of man, nothing save the principles and institutions which best accord with practice.[5]

A possible confusion of aims here appears: it is one thing to deduce a political theory from "the real nature of man," it is another to arrive at principles "which best accord with practice." How can Spinoza know that he will not arrive at "new or unheard of suggestions" if his inquiry is to be conducted, as in the same (Latin) sentence he says it will be, "with the same freedom of spirit as we generally use in mathematics"? [6] It is possible, of course, to save the sense of the passage as an enthymeme, taking Spinoza to mean that he will not deliberately seek novelty and that he will as far as possible adapt to each other the requirements of human nature and historically known political patterns or, that in some unexpressed way, common political patterns already contain important adaptations to the necessities of human nature.[7]

Because the alternative to constitutionalism is reliance on the wisdom and good intent of rulers and subjects, a constitution may be defined negatively as the refusal of such reliance; [8] positively, it will be best understood as the subjec-

---

[4] TP, I, par. 3; Aristotle *Politics* 1264a.

[5] TP, I, par. 4.

[6] TP (Dover), I, par. 4, 288. The Dover translation is preferred here. See Stuart Hampshire's criticism of Wernham's translation of this passage in *The Philosophical Quarterly*, pp. 80–83.

[7] In this statement of reliance on practice and the criticism of utopian planning, Spinoza's opening passage in the *Tractatus Politicus* bears striking and significant resemblances to Machiavelli, *The Prince*, Ch. XV, p. 56.

[8] TP, VII, par. 4.

tion of both ruler and subject to a public, constant, and rational law.[9]

What is the best constitution, and how is a constitution to be safeguarded?

When the safety of a state depends on any man's good faith, and its affairs cannot be administered properly unless its rulers choose to act from good faith, it will be very unstable; if a state is to be capable of lasting, its administration must be so organized that it does not matter whether its rulers are led by reason or passion— they cannot be induced to break faith or act badly. In fact it makes no difference to the stability of a state what motive leads men to conduct its affairs properly, provided that they *are* conducted properly. For freedom or strength of mind is a private virtue; the virtue of a state is stability.[10]

The two questions are one; the best constitution ("organization of the administration") is the same as the constitution which best preserves itself.[11] Again,

to arrange every detail of the constitution so that everyone, whatever his disposition, prefers public right to private advantage, this is the task and this the toil. Its urgency has forced men to devise many solutions; yet they have never succeeded in ensuring that the state ran less risk from its citizens than from external enemies.[12]

The principal danger to a constitution is from within the state; the purpose of the constitution maker is to establish a set of political arrangements which will exploit the existing passions of men [13] and yet achieve a rational end.[14] That is to say, "the problem of the formation of the state, hard as it may sound, is

---

[9] TP, II, par. 21. "Rational" here means "reasonable."
[10] TP, I, par. 6. As will be noted at greater length below, "stability" does not refer only to temporal endurance and absence of overt conflict.
[11] TP, X, par. 9.
[12] TTP, XVII, 153–55.
[13] TP, VII, par. 2; E, IV, prop. 37; Aristotle *Nichomachean Ethics* 1103a; Augustine *City of God* xix. 24; Deane, p. 141; Hume, pp. 538–39.
[14] TTP, IV, 69; TP, X, par. 9.

not insoluble, even for a race of devils, granted that they have intelligence." [15]

Spinoza believes, as we have said, that men's rational interests do not conflict, that there is a natural harmony of real human interests. Yet there is much actual conflict among men and so a political structure for the artificial harmonization of interests is a practical necessity. Because men falsely see their interests as mutually adverse, unending strife must follow unless a judiciously calculated system of laws so changes the conditions of choice that in seeking their own benefit, however narrowly conceived, men also work toward the benefit of all. [16]

Although the method of the artificial harmonization of interests is most clearly seen in the reward and punishment aspects of statute law, constitution makers must take into account a problem which is not vitally important in statute law: *quis custodiet ipsos custodes?* Spinoza adopts the methods of the division and balance of the power of making decisions, at the same time that he maintains the unity of the power that enforces decisions. Many interest groups must have an effective way of influencing decisions of state. This is not a theory of "mixed constitutions" as we find them in Polybius and Machiavelli. [17]

The general argument runs: The state is the condition necessary to civilized or rational life. The stability of the state is therefore a major aim of all men who understand their interests. The greatest danger to the stability of the state arises

[15] Kant, *Perpetual Peace*, p. 27.
[16] Simmel, pp. 13–17; Halévy, pp. 17–18, 489–92; TP, X, par. 6; TP, VII, par. 8; TP, VII, par. 4.
[17] TTP, XVII, 171. Spinoza's account of the Jewish state is a description of a balance of power; Hubbeling, p. 78: "This method of equilibrium is predominant in Spinoza's political philosophy"; and is similar to his idea of playing the emotions off against each other in the individual (TTP, XVI, 131). Hubbeling adds, at p. 81: "This concept of equilibrium was widespread in the seventeenth century. It was taken from the study of mechanics and applied in various fields"; Polybius *Histories* vi:10; Machiavelli, *Discourses*, I, Ch. 2, pp. 215–16.

from among its own subjects. Unrest among subjects is usually the fault of the sovereign or of the constitution.[18] A sovereign, whether one person or many, cannot be held accountable in Spinoza's deterministic system; all that can be "blamed" is the faulty system that chose the sovereign or gave it the kind of powers it has. The constitution, then, is "the soul of the state." [19] The chief aim of a political thinker is to devise and bring into effect a constitution which will not allow the sovereign to make serious mistakes and which will satisfy all elements of the populace which are capable in their dissatisfaction of weakening the state.[20] The ideal is rather workability than abstract justice. A good constitution will be like a homeostatic mechanism, so contrived as to use the forces that impinge upon it to maintain its own equilibrium; it will neither foolishly rely upon the virtue of subjects or rulers nor will it crush or fail to utilize what virtue exists; [21] it will draw strength both from the reasoned support and from the artificially channeled passions of subjects and rulers:

Now if human nature were such that men desired most what was most to their advantage, there would be no need of artifice to promote loyalty and concord. But since, as is well known, human nature is very different, it is necessary to organize the state so that all its members, rulers as well as ruled, do what the common welfare requires whether they wish to or not; that is to say, live in accordance with the precept of reason, either spontaneously or through force or necessity.[22]

[18] TP, V, par. 2; TP, VI, par. 6.
[19] TP, X, par. 9.
[20] TP, X, par. 8.
[21] Some recent writers on political theory have maintained that classical thought saw the state as the instrument for producing virtue in subjects, whereas later thought seeks only for political stability. Probably it is true that this later thought is more concerned with the political problem of passion and interest, yet what could be more evident than that Machiavelli, Spinoza, and Rousseau, to mention only a few, are interested in contriving states in which men will find salvation or virtue? On the other hand, the concept of the caretaker state, commonly ascribed to Hobbes or to nineteenth-century liberalism, goes back as far as to Augustine and Aristotle.
[22] TP, VI, par. 3.

Some commentators have been scornful of Spinoza's "paper constitutions" and of the "city of hucksters" [23] which he calls a state. They might, of course be correct in believing that the particular arrangements which he suggests would not work out as he intended. Their failure to take this line of argument, however, or to reply to his reasoning in defense of the institutional arrangements he sets forth, suggests a failure to read the text closely. On the face of matters, Spinoza should be the last one we should expect to write constitutions depending solely or excessively on the virtue or enlightened rationality of subjects or rulers. He says:

In laying down fundamental laws it is necessary to pay particular attention to human passions. To have shown what ought to be done is not enough; the main problem is to show how it can be done, *i.e.*, how men, even when led by passion, may still have fixed and stable laws. If civil right or public liberty, has no basis but the slender support of legal prescriptions, it will not only be very difficult for the citizens to maintain . . . but will prove their undoing.[24]

Spinoza never departs from this principle of relying on specified human passions in his proposed constitutions. Every institution is supported by an interest; groups of institutions form a pattern, mutually supportive, which it is to the interest of all, or almost all, to maintain.[25] Nor are these interests supposed to be those of a nation of philosophers. The interests mentioned are interests in money, in power, in glory, and in crude physi-

---

[23] Vaughan, *Studies*, pp. 93–94, 113, 117.

[24] TP, VII, par. 3. In his review of the Wernham translation, Hampshire argues that "civil right" should be translated as "the constitution" or "the force of law," and that "very difficult" should be rendered as "impossible." The Latin text (Wernham, p. 334) seems to support Hampshire's contention: "*Nam si imperii jura, sive libertas publica, solo invalido legum auxilio nitatus, non tantum nulla ejus obtinendae erit civibus securitas . . .*"

[25] Aristotle *Politics* 1270b: "If a constitution is to survive, all the elements of the state must join in willing its existence and its continuance."

cal self-preservation.[26] In speaking of the monarchical council he says:

But human nature is such that everyone pursues his private advantage with the greatest eagerness, regards the laws which he thinks necessary for the preservation and promotion of his own interests as entirely fair, and defends another's cause if—but only if—he believes that by so doing he is strengthening his own position. It is therefore necessary to appoint counsellors whose private interests and advantage are bound up with the general welfare and the maintenance of peace. So if some are chosen from each class or group of citizens, the measure which receives the most votes in their council will obviously be to the advantage of the majority of the subjects.[27]

The statement that "a constitution cannot be kept intact unless it is supported both by reason and by the common passions of men" [28] most succinctly expresses the necessities of constitution making: if the basic law is merely rational, "if it depends on the support of reason only, it is weak and easily overthrown," [29] whereas if it is itself an instrument only of men's passions, it will perish in the unmediated conflict of those passions.

Of the three model constitutions which he planned to set forth, Spinoza completed only two, the monarchic and the aristocratic. Of his two purposes, "to deduce from the real nature of man, nothing save the principles and institutions

---

[26] TP, VII, par. 3. As for money, for example, sometimes the desire for it is harnessed to the interest of the state, as at TP, VII, par. 21 and TP, VIII, par. 31, and sometimes the same desire must be defeated or frustrated, as at TP, VII, par. 13. There are circumstances under which greed for money should be encouraged, as at TP, X, par. 6 and TP, VII, par. 17: "The prevailing avarice of men is another reason for my plan; for the hire of mercenaries is bound to be expensive, and citizens find the exactions needed to maintain an idle soldiery very hard to bear."

[27] TP, VII, par. 4.

[28] TP, X, par. 9.

[29] *Ibid.*

which accord best with practice," [30] the first, the deduction from the real nature of man, is most methodically carried out; as for the appeal to practice, historical examples are used in the way in which Machiavelli used them, as illustrations rather than in the rigorous manner proposed: "we can confirm from actual experience that this form of monarchy is the best by surveying every civilized state and examining the causes of its preservation and downfall. But to do this would be extremely tedious for the reader." [31]

There is little point in reproducing the clear and detailed account which Spinoza gives of his model constitutions. They are treated of here only as illustrations and clarifications of his general political outlook.

Monarchy

Spinoza commences his study of monarchy with an attack on its more usual forms. The arrangement which entrusts the direction of all affairs to one man is a poor arrangement, even from the point of view of the interest of the king himself.[32] If he is incompetent, the subjects suffer; if he is competent, his interests are yet different from those of his subjects.[33] No one man can actually hold so much power and so monarchies are usually covert aristocracies, the worst kind of aristocracy.[34] The more concentrated a power is, the more easily it can be transferred by a *coup d'etat*.[35] Kings have a penchant for dynastic and other wars of a sort which have no

---

[30] TP, I, par. 4.

[31] TP, VII, par. 30.

[32] TP, VI, par. 8; TP, VII, par. 14: "the exercise of absolute power by a prince is most dangerous to himself."

[33] See Machiavelli, *Discourses*, II, Ch. 2, p. 362: "it is beyond question that it is only in republics that the common good is looked to properly."

[34] TP, VI, par. 5, which may be taken to be Spinoza's reply to Hobbes's remark that democracies are really a rule by orators; Geyl, II, 202–203: after 1672 the regents of the Netherlands continued to rule, but without responsibility.

[35] TP, VII, par. 14; TTP, n. 36, p. 251.

relevance to the interests of subjects;[36] governments which are not directed toward the interests of subjects do not receive their full support, and because this support is the sole strength of governments, despotic monarchies are necessarily weak.[37] Spinoza admits that such despotisms are often the most enduring of states, but says that duration alone is not a criterion of power and that peace is not mere absence of war but a union or agreement of minds.[38] With apparent direct reference to Hobbes, he remarks that the peace of despotism is the peace of a desert.[39]

These are some of the requirements of a constitutional monarchy:

The army must be recruited from the citizens alone, and no one must be exempted from military service.[40]

The fields and the whole territory—and if possible, the houses also—should be owned by the state, *i.e.*, by the sovereign; who should let them out at an annual rent to the citizens.[41]

Everyone . . . should be admitted to the citizen roll, and have his name inscribed on the roll of his tribe, as soon as he is old enough to bear arms and undergo military training; unless he is a convicted criminal, a mute, a lunatic, or a menial who supports himself by some servile occupation.[42]

A council is appointed by the king from lists submitted by each tribe of the kingdom. Something on the order of 2,000 members is contemplated, a third to a fifth of whom are to be replaced each year. The duty of the council is to advise the

[36] TP, VII, par. 24.

[37] TP, VII, par. 11; Geddes, at I, 443–44, notes a resemblance between the preceding arguments against ordinary monarchy and those given by Jan DeWitt in his "Deduction" of 1654, a defense of the Exclusion Act.

[38] TP, V, par. 4; TP, VI, par. 4.

[39] At TP, VII, par. 1, Spinoza argues that despotisms are not, by nature, stable. If they endure, it is by accident.

[40] TP, VI, par. 10; Aristotle *Politics* 1311a, "The guard of a king is a civic guard: the guard of a tyrant is a foreign guard of mercenary troops."

[41] TP, VI, par. 12; see also TP, VII, par. 8; TP, VII, par. 19.

[42] TP, VI, par. 11; see also TP, VI, par. 32: "It should be easy to become a citizen."

king, publish his ordinances, and supervise the administration. All petitions from citizens to the king, as well as all diplomatic correspondence from abroad, pass through the council. Ambassadors are also first received by the council. The full council meets perhaps four times a year, but fifty of its members are appointed to a standing committee for the handling of routine matters such as the supervision of the treasury. The king's ministers report to the council.[43]

Spinoza frankly states that the principal object of insisting on a citizen army is to restrain the tendency of a monarchy to slide into despotism.[44]

The surprising suggestion that the king own all real estate is not to be thought of as anticipatory of socialist or single-tax doctrines—Spinoza's economic "liberalism" is of the Adam Smith kind—but rather as harking back to a feudal theory that the sovereign is the ultimate owner of all lands and permanent improvements within the kingdom:[45]

Again, if there is one thing which an individual in the condition of nature cannot appropriate and make his own, it is land and other real estate. Thus the land and other real estate is essentially the public property of the commonwealth, i.e., it belongs by right to all who have united and are therefore able to protect it, or to the man whom they have all empowered to protect it for them.[46]

If we consider the vast amount of intellectual gossip in the seventeenth century, it seems unlikely that Spinoza was igno-

[43] TP, VI, par. 15–28.
[44] TTP, XVII, 173: "It is only by means of mercenary troops that rulers can oppress their peoples"; TP, VI, par. 34, where it is said that even the palace guard must be citizens and paid out of public funds, not out of the king's privy purse; TP, VII, par. 17: "It is also to ensure that the citizens retain possession of their own right, and preserve their freedom, that they alone must form the army . . . for an armed man is more fully possessed of his own right than one who is unarmed . . . citizens transfer their right to another completely, and commit it entirely to his good faith, as soon as they give him arms"; also, TP, VII, par. 22: "the supreme reward for military service is freedom."
[45] Ogg, pp. 309–10.
[46] TP, VII, par. 19.

rant of the theory of Harrington about the relation of forms of government to land ownership, but though he might be thought to follow Harrington's recommendations in his monarchical constitution, he disregards them in treating of aristocracy. It is certain that Spinoza knew of the communist proposals made by various Anabaptist sects, particularly the Mennonites, yet no extended or clear references to, or intimations of sympathy with, such programs appear in his writings. The objects which he most probably had in view were: the relief of the chronic poverty of kings and the elimination of the resulting need for oppressive, illegal, and uneconomic taxes; the desire to put all citizens on an equal footing in time of invasion; [47] and the suppression of the power of the landed nobility.[48]

The king's council is the central matter of interest in Spinoza's model monarchy. The details of the arrangements he suggests are, with some additions from English and French practice, taken mostly from actual Dutch political procedure. The king selects the councilors, but he does so from lists presented to him by the "tribes"; the lists need not contain the names of any of his supporters.[49] It is not clear just what is meant by the council's supervision of the treasury and the requirement that the king's ministers report to the council, but some considerable degree of control is implied. Perhaps the critical point is that subjects are "bound to obey all the commands or edicts of the king that have been published by the great council." [50] The provision clearly gives the council a

[47] The famous ability of the Netherlands to defend itself against invasion by flooding its land was often compromised, to the point of rebellion, by the resistance of land-owners whose land would be seriously damaged by the salt water; Renier, p. 194; Geyl, II, 123.

[48] Temple, II, 508.

[49] Geyl, II, 132–33; *CMH*, p. 279; Renier, p. 17. The relation between William III and the States General seems clearly to be the prototype of Spinoza's suggestions here.

[50] TP, VI, par. 39. Compare with the French practice of registering edicts with parlements.

veto on the enforcement, or even enactment, of any law proposed by the king.[51]

What if the king acts outside of or against the law?

If a monarchy is to be stable it must be organized so that everything is done by the king's decree alone (*i.e.*, every law is the king's declared will), but not everything the king wills is law.[52]

For the fundamental laws of the state must be regarded as the king's permanent decrees, so that his ministers render him complete obedience in refusing to execute any command of his which contravenes them.[53]

The final statement on monarchy is: "The people can maintain a fair amount of freedom under a king as long as it ensures that the king's power is determined by its power alone, and preserved only by its support." [54]

In view of the number and extent of the limitations on the royal power and the painstaking precautions against the corruption or intimidation of the council, it seems safe to say that Spinoza's monarch is little more than a figurehead, that his constitutional monarchy resembles the British constitution of the nineteenth more than it does that of the seventeenth century. But though the monarchical constitution is meant to "secure sovereignty for the king and freedom and peace for the citizens," [55] it is evident that it is the least favored of Spinoza's constitutions, that he had an abiding distrust of monarchy. "For what can kings bear less than to rule by courtesy, and to have their power restricted by another's?" [56] He was probably right in doubting that even his own mon-

---

[51] TP, VII, par. 5.
[52] TP, VII, par. 1.
[53] *Ibid.*
[54] TP, VII, par. 31.
[55] TP, VII, par. 15.
[56] TTP, XVII, 187; TTP, XVI, 139: "for who but a fool who knows nothing of the right of sovereigns will take at their face value the words and promises . . ."

archic constitution could have tamed a Stuart king, or a Louis XIV.

Aristocracy

Spinoza treats of two kinds of aristocracy: the centralized and the dispersed. Venice is the model of the first kind, the Netherlands of the second.

A departure is made from the standard distinction between aristocracy as the rule of the few and democracy as the rule of the many: "In an aristocracy the right to govern is entirely dependent on co-optation, whereas in a democracy it depends mainly on a kind of innate right, or a right acquired by fortune." [57]

That is, in an aristocracy, the new members are chosen by the present members, whereas in a democracy, citizenship is based on some rule, as age, birth, or financial contribution. The definitions are strange, in that according to them the usual understanding of democracy and aristocracy could be reversed. The hereditary aristocracy of history is now to be called a democracy; there could be a state which would fit Spinoza's definition of aristocracy in which a majority, or even every one of the citizens, are aristocrats.[58]

In fact, the aristocracies and the democracy which Spinoza actually considers are not exotic types. The democracy he discusses is very broadly based. In an actual aristocracy he recognizes that the rulers will have an interest in limiting membership and will generally co-opt their own children or nearest of kin, although there should be no law against the selection of qualified plebeians.[59] The aristocracies Spinoza sets forth are what we would call commercial oligarchies. Nowhere does he treat of a landed aristocracy, much less consider how it might be made a rational system. This is not an

---

[57] TP, VIII, par. 1.
[58] *Ibid.*, par. 14; TP, XI, par. 2; Aristotle *Politics* 1290a, b.
[59] TP, VIII, par. 2; Boxer, p. 41.

oversight on his part, though Europe had lived and still in his time mostly lived under such a system. For Spinoza, Hobbes, and most seventeenth-century intellectuals, the feudal aristocratic system, the "gothic system," was not a system at all but a confusion, a barbarism.

Each member of the aristocracy is a lifetime member of the ruling council. Spinoza says that "everything the council wills is law, without exception," [60] and that "in determining the fundamental laws of aristocracy we must make sure above all that they rest solely on the will and power of the supreme council." [61] The common people have no part in government. [62]

The supreme council cannot be limited as a monarch can be—there is no power strong enough to contend with the united aristocrats and so no constitutional function can be given to those outside of the aristocracy who have no power to enforce their rights. The only method of maintaining an aristocratic state is by the division of the aristocracy itself in such a way that one part will restrain another, while all parts unite to maintain the common class interests.

Spinoza's aristocracy can better maintain its class unity because each member derives his political power solely from his membership in the council; his interest will thus always lie in maintaining the power of the council rather than his own power against that of the council. [63]

The system of state ownership of land will not be attempted in the aristocratic model. If the common people have no stake in the country they are likely to leave it in time of

[60] TP, VIII, par. 4.

[61] Ibid., par. 7.

[62] Ibid., par. 9. In only one of Spinoza's model governments, the aristocratic, do the common people play no part, or no constitutional part. See also TP, VIII, pars. 44, 45 where it is said that the right (power) of the people must be reduced to a minimum. Even the right of economic association must be restrained.

[63] Ibid., par. 19.

war or hardship.[64] The army may consist of citizens or of paid mercenaries—there is no point in specifying which, because there is no power in the state capable of enforcing either requirement.[65]

The most important requirement for a successful aristocracy is that its membership be large. If the number of patricians be very small, say two or three, the state will be composed of that many factions.[66] Spinoza calculates that scarcely three in a hundred patricians are likely to have any ability to govern; it follows that if a hundred men are needed to govern, that the aristocracy must include at least 5,000 adult males. Another way of looking at it would fix the proportion of patricians to plebeians at one to fifty as a minimum.[67]

Further requirements of a successful aristocracy are: equality among the patricians,[68] maintenance of the superiority of patricians over plebeians, unity of the patrician class,[69] efficiency in government, and regard to the general welfare. The necessary concentration of power in the council need

give the common people no cause to fear any danger of slavery and oppression. For the will of so large a council must be determined by reason rather than by caprice; since evil passions draw men in different directions, and they can be guided as if by one mind only in so far as they aim at ends which are honorable, or at any rate appear to be so.[70]

The power of the council is not, and cannot be, constitutionally limited in any way, but the necessary division of

[64] *Ibid.*, par. 10.

[65] *Ibid.*, par. 9. The Netherlands employed mercenaries.

[66] *Ibid.*, par. 1; Aristotle *Politics* 1306b.

[67] *Ibid.*, pars. 2, 13; TP, IX, par. 14: "the sudden overthrow of the republic was not due to time wasted on deliberations, but to its defective condition and the fewness of its rulers."

[68] TP, IX, par. 8; TP, VIII, par. 9.

[69] TP, VIII, par. 19; Aristotle *Politics* 1308a; *CMH*, p. 276, discord within the regent class, after 1664, paralyzed provincial government.

[70] TP, VIII, par. 6; Rousseau, *Social Contract*, Bk. I, Ch. 3, p. 26.

power is accomplished by creating, within the council, a smaller council of older men, called syndics, "whose sole duty shall be to see that the state laws concerning the assemblies are kept unbroken," [71] and

that all the laws of the state which are absolutely fundamental may remain in force forever, it must be laid down that if anyone calls in question any fundamental law in the supreme council—moves, for example, that the command of some general should be extended, or that the number of patricians should be diminished, or the like—he should be arraigned for high treason.[72]

The impression that the syndics are an institution on the order of a Supreme Court is not warranted, however, in view of the sentence which follows the last one quoted above:

But to strengthen the other general laws of the state it is enough to enact that no law can be repealed, or a new one made, unless first the council of syndics, and then three-fourths or four-fifths of the supreme council have agreed to it.[73]

We learn further than the syndics have "the right to summon the supreme council, and to bring up matters for its decision," [74] and,

Finally, the common people too will be sufficiently protected if they are allowed to appeal to the syndics, who, as I have said, should be permitted by law to hear evidence, decide, and pronounce judgement on the proceedings of the judges. For there is no doubt that while the syndics will be unable to avoid the hatred of many patricians, they will always be very popular with the common people, and will do everything they possibly can to win its applause.[75]

[71] TP, VIII, par. 20. Cf. Aristotle's criticism of the ephoralty, *Politics* 1270b.
[72] TP, VIII, par. 25. The history of this constitutional safeguard in the classical world does not inspire confidence in its efficacy.
[73] *Ibid.*
[74] TP, VIII, par. 26.
[75] TP, VIII, par. 41.

Spinoza goes on to discuss the dispersed aristocracy. This state is a union of cities, each of which has some capacity for autonomy and self-defense and each of which is a little aristocratic state in itself, complete with council and syndics, an army, a system of taxation, and control over all local matters.[76]

The central government of the dispersed aristocracy consists of a senate which settles disputes between cities. Each city is represented in the senate in proportion to its relative strength as measured by its population. Taxes are assessed by the senate on the member cities;[77] there will also be a federal body of syndics. The important matter of how the federal senate or body of syndics enforce their decisions is not discussed.

The superiority of dispersed over centralized aristocracy derives from its relative immunity from revolution or sudden attack from without.[78] Other cities will join to assist against local uprisings or invasions. The individual city of a federation of cities is likely to extend better treatment to its plebeians because its representation in the central government is relative to its total population; patricians will do all they can to retain their subjects and to attract more.[79]

Spinoza agrees with Machiavelli that all forms of government are subject to gradual decay.[80] Machiavelli's solution was the institution of the dictatorship. The function of the dictator is to act as a new hero-founder, to bring the state back to

[76] TP, IX, par. 5.

[77] *Ibid.*, par. 8.

[78] TP, X, par. 10; TP, IX, par. 15; Rousseau, *Social Contract*, Bk. III, Ch. 13, p. 91.

[79] TP, IX, par. 14; de la Court, p. 57; Spinoza seems to agree with Rousseau that a growing population is a sign of good government; Boxer, p. 19, remarks that Amsterdam was built up partly by refugees from Antwerp; Zumthor, p. 261: "In 1685, a Frenchman calculated that the number of foreigners or descendants of foreigners with established homes in the province of Holland amounted to half the total population"; see also, Rousseau, *Social Contract*, Bk. III, Ch. 9, p. 83, and Machiavelli, *Discourses*, II, Ch. 3, p. 365.

[80] TP, IX, par. 1; Machiavelli, *Discourses*, III, Ch. 1, p. 459.

its original principles and then to hand his power back to the ordinary authorities. Spinoza rejects this remedy [81] on the ground that the natural leaning of an aristocracy toward monarchy, combined with the ambitions of the dictator and the presumably decayed state of the constitution, will result in the final end of the aristocratic form. Furthermore, the suggested body of syndics is already a kind of mild, permanent dictatorship, yet they cannot, because they are themselves necessarily involved in it, arrest the slow moral rot that undermines states. The only solution to the problem raised by the gradual erosion of civic spirit in established states is by the method of framing the laws to harness even the minor passions to the interests of the state. Ambition, for example, should be positively directed to the service of the community rather than allowed to degenerate into competitive ostentation. [82]

The order in which Spinoza presents his model constitutions is also an order of increasing value, and of increasing absoluteness. By "absoluteness," Spinoza means the ability of a government to do what it wishes. Because government is a good thing, the more effective a government can be, the more absolute it is, the better it is. He judges aristocracy to be more absolute than monarchy, and democracy more absolute than aristocracy. [83] It is possible that Spinoza was looking too closely at the particular situation in the Netherlands, where a small dispersed aristocracy had defeated monarchical Spain. His model monarchical state can in part be understood as a suggestion to the House of Orange, which at the time of his writing the *Tractatus Politicus* was engaged in consolidating its rule; his dispersed aristocracy is a model of how the system

---

[81] Even Machiavelli has reservations: *Discourses*, I, Ch. 18, p. 261.

[82] TP, X, par. 6; Rousseau, *Political Writings*, p. 229, but, Aristotle *Politics* 1271a.

[83] TP, VIII, par. 4; the reassurance at TP, VIII, par. 6 seems weak and may be contradicted at TP, VII, par. 17; TP, VIII, par. 7, with which Temple (I, 24), disagrees; Spinoza may not have seen that although the united aristocrats are stronger than the king, in his models, the aristocracy may yet be weaker than the monarchy.

that ended with the murder of Jan DeWitt in 1672 might have been remodeled to work and to survive. Despite his criticisms of details, Spinoza's sympathies, between the two regimes, are decidedly on the side of DeWitt republicanism or aristocracy,[84] but he seems not to have realized how special were the circumstances that permitted that peculiar set of arrangements to survive and how difficult it is to assimilate it to any of the standard constitutions.[85]

The objection to characterizing even the dispersed form of aristocracy as more absolute than the model monarchy lies also in its own incoherence, particularly in such matters as the role of the syndics, and also in its evasion of the problem of furnishing adequate protection to the interests of the plebeians. The government must go in fear of its subjects because no adequate channel for their discontents can be provided. Disruptive conflicts within such a state, of the kind that actually occurred in the Netherlands, seem inevitable.[86]

Spinoza's defense of the DeWitt regime and of dispersed aristocracy has been mistaken for a shift from the preference for democracy evinced in the *Tractatus Theologico-Politicus* to a preference for aristocracy in the *Tractatus Politicus*. As we shall show, only the most casual reading could bring about such a belief; a more exact study of the text shows quite the opposite.

Democracy

The incompleted *Tractatus Politicus* contains less than a hundred Latin lines of the text of that section which was to describe an effective democratic constitution. We have, therefore, almost no idea of how Spinoza proposed to organize his model democratic state. A collection of all the references to

---

[84] TP, VIII, par. 44.
[85] Spinoza's defense of extreme decentralism is partly a defense of the DeWitt policy, but also is derived from his own belief that a pluralist system of competing units is always to be preferred.
[86] TP, VIII, pars. 4, 5.

democracy in his writings serves to establish his preference for that form of government both as a matter of personal prefer- ence and as an expression of his systematic political thought, but does almost nothing to tell us how he thought democracy might be made to work in practice.

Democracy is "defined as a general assembly of men that possesses in its corporate capacity the supreme right to do everything it can." [87] It is a state where "all decide by common consent to live only by the dictates of reason." [88]

I have shown that in a democracy (which comes nearest to the natural condition) all make a covenant to act, but not to judge and think, in accordance with the common decision; that is, because all men cannot think alike, they agree that the proposal which gets the most votes shall have the force of a decree, but meanwhile retain the authority to revoke such decrees when they discover better. Thus, the less freedom of judgement men are allowed, the greater is the departure from the most natural con- dition, and, in consequence, the more oppressive is the govern- ment.[89]

Democracy is defended against the claims of monarchy, that is, against the House of Orange and the political program of Hobbes: In the Hebrew state,

as long as the people held the kingdom, there was only one civil war . . . But after the people, though quite unused to kings, changed the state into a monarchy, there was almost no end to civil wars.[90]

Finally, as long as the people continued to rule, the laws re- mained uncorrupted and were observed with great constancy . . . Nor do we hear of the people being deceived by false prophets until after the sovereignty was given to kings . . . Moreover, the people . . . found it easy to reform itself . . . whereas the kings,

[87] TTP, XVI, 133.
[88] TTP, XIX, 209.
[89] TTP, XX, 239.
[90] TTP, XVIII, 195.

with the unvarying self-confidence of royalty, and its inability to give way without loss of face, persisted obstinately in their faults right down to the final destruction of the city.[91]

Clearly, then, a whole people will never transfer its right to one man or a few if its members can agree among themselves.[92]

The claims of aristocracy are similarly refuted and a democratic system is again preferred:

liberty and the common good perish when a few men decide everything to suit their own whims. The fact is that human wits are too blunt to get to the heart of all problems immediately; but they are sharpened by the give and take of discussion and debate and by exploring every possible course men eventually discover the measures they wish, measures which all approve and which no one would have thought of before the discussion.[93]

Again,

if patricians were such that they could divest themselves of all partiality in choosing their colleagues, and be guided only by zeal for the public welfare, there would be no state to compare with aristocracy. But the very opposite is the case, as actual experience has amply shown.[94]

In direct defense of democracy, it

seemed to be the most natural form of state and to come nearest to preserving the freedom which nature allows to the individual. For in it no one transfers his natural right to another so completely that he is never consulted again, but each transfers it to a majority of the whole community of which he is a member. In

[91] *Ibid.*, p. 197. Cf. Machiavelli, *Discourses*, I, Ch. 58, p. 342.

[92] TP, VII, par. 5; see also TTP (Dover), Pref., p. 5; TP, V, par. 7; TP, VI, par. 4: "So it is slavery, not peace, that is furthered by the transfer of all power to one man."

[93] TP, IX, par. 14. This passage also shows Spinoza's commitment to empiricism in practical politics. A good philosopher might make a poor political scientist.

[94] TP, XI, par. 2.

this way, all remain equal, as they were before in the condition of nature.[95]

There is less danger of foolish decrees in a democracy: first because it is practically impossible for the majority in an assembly, especially in a large assembly, to agree upon a piece of folly; and secondly because of the basis and aim of democracy, which, as I have also shown, is precisely to avoid the follies of appetite and to restrain men as far as possible within the bounds set by reason, that they may live in harmony and peace.[96]

The apparent unequal ability of men in political matters does not reflect their actual capacity:

everyone is fairly competent and shrewd in matters to which he has long applied himself with enthusiasm.[97]

All men have one and the same nature: it is power and culture that mislead us . . . they are kept in ignorance of the main affairs of state and can merely guess at the facts.[98]

Men should really be governed in such a way that they do not regard themselves as being governed at all, but as following their own bent and their own free choice in their manner of life; in such a way then, that they are restrained only by love of freedom, desire to increase their possessions, and the hope of obtaining offices of state.[99]

It is true that no states

have proved so short-lived and so liable to constant civil strife as popular or democratic states. But if slavery, barbarism, and desolation are to be called peace, peace is the greatest misfortune that men can suffer.[100]

In this last phrase we see the distance between the political outlooks of Spinoza and of Hobbes, as well as the improbabil-

---

[95] TTP, XVI, 137; see also Rousseau, *Social Contract*, Bk. I, Ch. 6, pp. 13–14.
[96] TTP, XVI, 135. Cf. Machiavelli, *Discourses*, I, Ch. 4, p. 219.
[97] TP, VII, par. 4.
[98] TP, VII, par. 27.
[99] TP, X, par. 8.
[100] TP, VI, par. 4; Machiavelli, *Discourses*, I, Ch. 6, p. 225.

ity of the charge against Spinoza of quietism. We have seen Spinoza's opinion to be that the better the state, the more absolute it is; "the greater the right of the sovereign the more does the form of the state agree with the dictate of reason." [101] Democracy is the form of state which agrees most closely with the dictate of reason: "I come at length to the third and completely absolute state which we call democracy." [102]

Spinoza's definition of democracy, as has been noted, allows the name even to a government in which only the rich are admitted to citizenship if the general rule is that all who have a certain amount of wealth are citizens,[103] nor is even this odd kind of democracy necessarily inferior to aristocracy.[104] Yet, although many kinds of democracy are possible, Spinoza intended in the exposition which he never wrote

to confine myself to the type in which absolutely everyone who is bound only by the laws of his country, and is otherwise independent, and who leads a decent life, has the right to vote in the supreme council and to undertake offices of state.[105]

In the next few sentences we learn that those who are excluded are: aliens, women, children, servants, and those "who have gained a bad reputation through crime or some dishonorable mode of living." The monarchical constitution admits to citizenship "all the city-dwellers and farmers" and excludes only those who are also excluded in a democracy.[106] The democracy admits to citizenship "all who are of citizen parentage, or who have been born within the fatherland, or who have done good service to the commonwealth." [107]

---

[101] TP, VIII, par. 7.
[102] TP, XI, par. 1.
[103] TP, XI, par. 2. An emphasis on this point would bring Spinoza's democracy close to Locke's property-state.
[104] *Ibid.*, "We shall find little to choose between them."
[105] TP, XI, par. 3.
[106] TP, VI, par. 11. See TP, VIII, par. 14, for similar regulations on admission to the patriciate in an aristocracy.
[107] TP, XI, par. 1.

The most striking aspect of these voting qualifications, for the seventeenth century, is their silence on property or income. It is true that the term "servants" (*servos*) was taken more broadly at that time and might well include anyone who worked at the direction of another. Even taken at its broadest signification, however, the word did not include, in the Netherlands or in England, a great many small farmers or poor artisans. Some light is thrown on the matter by a consideration of the fourth section of Chapter XI of the *Tractatus Politicus*, where the question of whether women should have the vote is discussed solely in terms of the question of whether they are subject to men by nature or by convention.[108] In a logical order, the unwritten fifth section would have dealt with the question of whether servants could be citizens. We know that Spinoza did not regard the poorer classes as inferior by nature; it seems likely, therefore, that his exclusion of servants from full citizenship was based on the principle that they were too much subject to the influence of their masters. This, in turn, seems to relate more to body-servants than to commercial or industrial employees. It should be recalled that by the phrase "inferior by nature" Spinoza can mean nothing but "having less power."

All the evidence points to Spinoza's democracy as a direct democracy; there are several references to the "right to vote in the supreme council," none to voting for delegates or representatives as happens in the monarchical constitution.[109]

---

[108] TP, XI, par. 4.
[109] TTP, V, 95: "democracy; which is accordingly defined as a general assembly of men"; TTP, XX, 227–29: "a democracy where all or most men are colleagues in the government."

VIII

The State

❖

The Nature of the State

THE state is, for Spinoza, the chief mechanism for the forwarding of men's interests, but it is never more than a mechanism.[1] This utilitarian approach is, however, broadly conceived. As men's interests are served not merely by "circulation of the blood and other vital processes common to all animals, but primarily by reason, the true virtue and life of the mind," [2] so the state is a means of safeguarding not only those vital processes but also of enabling men "to exercise their mental and physical powers in safety and to use their reason freely." [3]

Of course Spinoza's attitude toward the nature of the state must be distinguished from that of those who also regard it as a human artifact but one which is suited to casual tinkering. To a degree which is almost Burkean, Spinoza recognizes that although man has created the state, the state has also created man, that it makes for him a second nature, that, in fact, in a sense which the organic political thinkers of the nineteenth century found overwhelmingly convincing, the state is prior to the individual. Spinoza recognizes the force of this insight and to a considerable extent accepts it, but the view he had of the power of the individual human understanding to cut through social conditioning and come to grips with objective

[1] TTP, III, 55; TdIE, p. 6; E, II, ax. 2.
[2] TP, V, par. 5.
[3] TTP, XX, 231.

reality enables him to circumvent the usual organic consequences. Of course most men do not exercise their understanding very much and so the state is to that extent somewhat organic in relation to them. It is never organic in itself. It is, in a derivative sense, an expression of the rational order of the universe, but it is an abstraction, not a system superordinate to its components—it has no urge to self-preservation, for instance.

The patterns which Spinoza discerns in the history of states are patterns derived from individual psychology rather than from any laws of the nature of the state itself. "Surely it is not peoples but individuals that nature creates." [4]

Purpose of the State

The initial purpose of the state is "secure and comfortable living," "peace and security of life," and "to remove general fear and to dispel general suffering." [5] It thus serves the interests of man as a merely living creature. As a particular kind of creature, one whose essence is understanding, man's interests are also served by government because "the purpose of the state is really freedom." [6] By freedom is meant both political freedom and the freedom of individual salvation; even in his nonpolitical works Spinoza recognizes the importance of good political organization to the search by the individual for autonomy. [7]

It has been noted that the more "absolute" the state is the more capable it is of attaining its rational ends and the more likely it is to do so, i.e., the better it is. There is no danger of the state becoming too strong, too absolute, nor does it ever make sense to speak of limiting the power of the state in the

---

[4] TTP, XVII, 181.
[5] TTP, III, 57; TP, V, par. 2; TP, III, par. 6.
[6] TTP, XX, 231.
[7] E, IV, prop. 73; TdIE, p. 7; compare argument at TTP, IV, 71–73, with Aristotle *Politics* 1252a.

interest of freedom.[8] The power of the state consists in its capacity for eliciting the support of its subjects; it cannot do this successfully unless it actually serves their interests.[9]

This point casts some light on the classic argument between the supporters of liberty and the supporters of authority. What appears to be a contention about the proper powers of the state may really be about the proper activities of the state. Spinoza, whose best state was also the most absolute state, did not believe that all of its actions were for the best: "It is one thing to cultivate a field by right, and another to cultivate it in the best way."[10]

Yet only in psychiatric wards is the Biblical advice to cut off offending members taken literally. It may be rational to destroy one government in order to substitute another, or to advocate that the government act differently or, in a certain sphere, not at all; it never makes sense to limit the power of government in general in order to preserve the illusory freedom of the state of nature.

Totalitarian governments are sometimes called absolute, but this usage does not correspond to that of Spinoza. Such states are sometimes best understood to be in the hero-founder stage of development, forced to use clumsy means of securing obedience because no other means are available. We ought, therefore, to be careful in applying Spinoza's remark:

It is not, I say, the purpose of the state to change men from rational beings into brutes and puppets; but rather to enable them to exercise their mental and physical powers in safety and use their reason freely.[11]

This statement could be taken to constitute an attack on some despotic regimes but not on new hero-founder states, for the

[8] TP, V, par. 1; TP, II, par. 17; TTP, XVII, 151.
[9] TP, V, par. 3.
[10] TP, V, par. 1.
[11] TTP, XX, 229.

evident reason that in them the subjects are brutes or puppets to begin with.

As the most useful thing to man is man, so the state is the most effective vehicle of that usefulness. Yet, although the state is instituted and maintained for the good of all, it cannot produce that good out of nowhere or suddenly. The state can afford to be only slightly more rational than the mass of its subjects; it will sometimes fall below even that level. The dead weight of general apathy and superstition has varied greatly throughout the course of history, but at no time has a statesman who appealed only or mainly to rational motives been able to accomplish his end or maintain his influence.[12] "A man cannot be ordered to be wise";[13]

simplicity and integrity of spirit are not inspired in men by the command of laws or by public authority, and it is quite impossible to make anyone blessed by force or legal enactments; the means required are pious and brotherly counsel, a good upbringing, and, above all, a judgement that is free and independent.[14]

The State in History

Spinoza had hopes for the future of mankind, hopes based on the diffusion of rationality through science (which is understood to include what we call philosophy), a higher standard of living, release from religious intolerance and superstition, free speech and improved political arrangements.[15] Nevertheless his writings are melioristic rather than utopian. He is the advocate, not of the perfect, but of the better state; the best state is, for him, the best one possible under given circumstances. We may distinguish two kinds of political program in his writings, the first explicit, the second implicit. In the first instance, given a people such as existed in Spinoza's time or in

[12] TP, X, par. 9.
[13] TTP (Dover), XIII, 178.
[14] TTP, VII, 109.
[15] But, TTP (Dover), Pref., p. 5.

our own, the better state would provide maximum security with minimum fear, would divert the passionate energies of men most effectively to the service of the common welfare, and would not positively hinder the ascent of individuals toward personal freedom. The implicit program envisions a people so completely ruled by the rational apprehension of the community of their interests that the state as a coercive force would wither away.[16]

These two ideal conditions may be taken to be the final pair of a series of five political conditions of man which Spinoza considers: (a) pre-rational man in the state of nature; (b) the man of the hero-founder state; (c) most states of Spinoza's and of classic and modern times, characterized by the routinization of political procedures and the stabilization of national characters and also by conflict and inefficiency resulting from the lack of understanding of political realities; (d) a rational state operating under one of the three constitutions suggested in the *Tractatus Politicus;* (e) the post-political condition of reasonable men.[17]

The importance of distinguishing among these stages of political development lies in the fact that Spinoza's scattered remarks on various issues often relate to different stages. If we are to understand his intent, it is sometimes necessary to ascertain which condition he is discussing. One of the errors which

[16] TTP, V, 93; XVI, 131; TP, VI, par. 3; III, par. 6; V, par. 5; TTP (Dover), XV, 199. Also, E, IV, prop. 37; Duff, p. 249: a supremely righteous state is the Kingdom of God on earth; p. 245: socialized men have no need of the state; Hallett, *Creation, Emanation and Salvation,* pp. 112–13: "The civic State itself, though no expression or abstraction of the *civitas Dei* . . ." yet contains it latently. The thought is, in part, that although the civic state may help to increase the number of saints in the *civitas Dei,* it is not itself that "city"; it cannot be more than instrumental.

[17] Hallett, *Creation, Emanation and Salvation,* p. 175: "that development is from barbarity to civility under sanctions, from civility to morality under obedience to obligations, or conscience, and from morality to perfection under enlightenment;" In the progression to the last condition, the terms "good man" and "good citizen" became synonymous; Aristotle *Politics* 1288a.

can arise out of inattentiveness to the context is the ascription
to Spinoza of an enthusiasm for the hero-founder stage, and an
emphasis on "public virtue," which would more suitably be
attributed to Machiavelli, or even to Rousseau.

The above described development from a state of nature
through political organization to noncoercive organization is,
for man, properly evaluated as a progress, and one in which
probably no step could be omitted. There is, however, no hint
in Spinoza's writings that progress is necessary or inevitable,
unless we are to take as such his remark that the force of the
intellect, though very weak as compared with the force of the
passions, is yet steadier than they and in time does more.[18]
Perhaps we may find an implicit political optimism in the fact
of Spinoza's writing about politics at all, given his theory of
personal salvation.

There are, it is true, intimations in his writings of what
seems to be a cyclical theory of history. At one place he
mentions the tendency of democracies to evolve into aristocracy and then into monarchy.[19] At another he seems to approve Machiavelli's theory of a natural cycle of civic morality.[20] In both cases, however, Spinoza shows that proper measures can halt the downward slide; clearly he does not think
that cyclical theories describe anything but possibilities.

Political stagnation at a very low level is of course possible.
Neither his distaste for despotic regimes nor his belief that
they are inherently unstable, blinds Spinoza to the fact that
they have often been of long continuance. They endure by
the use of their slight strength for the corruption of their
subjects and by the chance of proximity to equally feeble
regimes. There is a hint that the endless succession of such
regimes, caught in the cycle of poverty, apathy, and superstition, is more likely to be interrupted by external influences
than by the weak rational power of degraded subjects.

[18] E, V, prop. 7.
[19] TP, VIII, par. 12.
[20] TP, X, par. 1.

It has been said that "Spinoza greatly underestimates both the extent to which beliefs can be controlled and also man's capacity to abandon the power to reason freely." [21] He cannot be said to have ignored the problem:

one man's power of judgement can be subject to the right of a second in another way: the first man may be the dupe of the second.[22]

Admittedly a man's judgement can be influenced in many ways, some of them hardly credible; so much so, in fact that though not directly under another's command it may depend entirely upon his words, and thus in that respect can properly be called subject to his right.[23]

The paragraph continues:

Yet in spite of all that political skill has been able to achieve in this field, it has never been completely successful; men have always found that individuals were full of their own ideas, and that opinions varied as much as tastes.[24]

In general,

Could thought be controlled as easily as speech, all governments would rule in safety, and none would be oppressive; for everyone would live as his rulers wanted, and his judgements of true and false, good and bad, fair and unfair, would be determined entirely by their will. However, . . . it is impossible for thought to be completely subject to another's control, because no one can give up to another his natural right to reason freely and form his own judgement about everything, nor can he be compelled to do so.[25]

Once again, we see here the vital importance of Spinoza's metaphysics to his political thought. If he had accepted the

[21] Plamenatz, I, 80.
[22] TP, II, par. 11.
[23] TTP, XX, 227.
[24] Ibid.
[25] Ibid.; Perhaps in relation to individuals, Spinoza did underestimate the possibility of subjection to the will of another. Whether, to what extent, and for how long, a whole people can be so subjected is still, despite the gloomy prognostications recently current, an open question.

doctrine that man's rational thought deals only with the interconnections of words, that a thinking man is but juggling the
products of his own subjective imagination, he would, despite
their difference on natural right, have come to the same political conclusion at which Hobbes arrived.[26] The completely
dismal character of that conclusion, particularly as applied to
modern conditions, is somewhat obscured by Hobbes's evasive-
ness and by the persuasiveness of his incomparable literary
style. If Spinoza, with his greater clarity and commitment to
naturalism, and with his homely, plodding Latin, had come to
Hobbes's conclusions . . .

[26] Bidney, p. 91.

IX

Spinoza and Hobbes

❖

PARTLY because of the importance of their actual relationship and partly because of the expectations raised by current understandings of the history of political theory, a separate discussion of the agreements and disagreements between the political outlooks of Hobbes and Spinoza is a practical necessity.

Although a considerable fraction of their writings have to do with religious matters, both Spinoza and Hobbes have a completely secular outlook. They agree further in the rejection of the doctrine of free will, of natural law as understood by classical or medieval writers, and of the appeal to authority or custom in philosophy. Both accept radical individualism, egoistic psychology, naturalistic ethics, and the belief that the basic premises of the new physical sciences, as they understood them, were relevant to the study of political questions.[1] Both claim to derive their political outlooks from a study of human nature.[2] They agree further on the principle of the indivisibility of sovereign power, particularly with respect to religious claims, and on the importance of stability in government.

Given these and many other massive concordances, we should expect Spinoza's political thought to be at least somewhat similar to that of Hobbes. In what may be considered its preliminary passages, it is more than similar, it is identical, but

[1] Oakeshott, Introduction to *Leviathan*, pp. xxii–xxiii, to the contrary.
[2] TP, I, par. 7; Hobbes, *De Cive*, p. 3.

identical not so much with what Hobbes actually said as with
what he should have said had he been consistent. This may
seem strange language to use of England's most rigorous political philosopher, but in what follows it is hoped to show that
Spinoza was a more consistent Hobbist than Hobbes and,
further, to make plain the importance to an understanding of
Hobbes of some acquaintance with the criticism of his
younger contemporary.

In Hobbes's state of nature, the individual has the right to
do all things which are necessary, in his own opinion, for
self-preservation.[3] Spinoza, starting from similar premises,
argues that that right is not so limited but is a right to all
without qualification.

Hobbes's argument runs thus: Men in the state of nature
have a right to do all that is necessary for self-preservation
and, when self-preservation is not in question,[4] they have a
duty to observe the laws of nature. Because the laws of nature
are only the laws of self-preservation through peace with
other men, it appears that men have a general and unlimited
right to preserve themselves, on the one hand, and on the
other a special duty to preserve themselves in a particular way
when that way does not conflict with the prior general right.
Whether that duty is to actual performance or merely to
pious intent does not concern us here; the question is, how
Hobbes arrives at duty at all. If the laws of nature are to be
followed because they lead to preservation, and if man preserves himself, as Hobbes puts it, "as a stone falls," then they
will most certainly be followed, if known, and a "duty" to
observe them is redundant. If these laws are "conclusions
understood by reason," [5] then they are not duties but counsels

[3] Hobbes, De Cive, p. 56.
[4] Wernham, pp. 14–15; Is it ever not in question? Disregarding, as we
often must, what Hobbes should have thought, we find that he believed it
often was not in question, as when men act out of vanity, for example.
[5] Hobbes, De Cive, p. 59.

of prudence.[6] They cannot be obligatory as commands of God,[7] because his commands are not known in the state of nature.[8] Finally, if Hobbes elsewhere bases a duty on a promise, express or implied, he cannot do so here: there are no promises given to keep the law of nature; vows, or promises to oneself, are never binding; there are no parties in the state of nature between whom promises of a binding character can be exchanged. Hobbes is therefore not entitled to put limits on men's right in the state of nature. A right can be limited only by incapacity or by duty.

That Hobbes's thought nevertheless logically arrives at Spinoza's might-makes-right conclusion[9] is shown elsewhere rather clearly. Hobbes speaks of God, who

hath a right to rule, and to punish those who break his laws, from his sole irresistible power. For all right over others is either from nature, or from contract . . . Now if any man had so far exceeded the rest in power, that all of them with joined forces could not have resisted him, there had been no cause why he should part with that right which nature had given him . . . they therefor whose power cannot be resisted, and by consequence God Almighty, derives his right of sovereignty from the power itself.[10]

Here the right is not to all which is necessary to self-preservation, but to all that is possible; the right is not reserved to God only, but belongs to any man powerful enough to

[6] And so many commentators understand Hobbes to mean by "duty" only "prudence." Undoubtedly this is what he should mean, given his preceding ideas, but the belief that this is what he does mean is based on an interpretation rather than on a reading of the text.

[7] Warrender, p. 98, seems alone in holding the opinion that the laws of nature are obligatory because they are commands of God.

[8] If they were commands of God, and not known to be such, then, according to Hobbes, they would not be laws. A law, if it is to be a law, must originate from a known authority.

[9] Unless we can understand Hobbes to be saying, "I must, therefore I ought."

[10] Hobbes, De Cive, pp. 177–78.

hold it. Retelling the story of Job, Hobbes explains that the power of God (and therefore of any very powerful man) is self-justifying and not limited by any reference to morality: "God by his right might have made men subject to diseases and death, although they had never sinned, even as he hath made the other animals mortal and sickly, although they cannot sin." [11]

This is precisely the doctrine of Spinoza: "For since God has the right to do everything, and God's right is simply *God's power* conceived as completely free, it follows that each thing in nature has as much right from nature as it has power to exist and act." [12]

When he comes to treat of civil society, the relatively small problem of the place of duty in the state of nature becomes, for Hobbes, a great problem. The duty to obey the law of nature is replaced, in civil society, by the duty to obey the civil laws. The subject must obey these laws not only because the sovereign will punish him if he does not, but also because the duty to seek peace through the natural law has now become the duty to keep the peace through the observance of the civil law. In addition, the subject has entered into a double obligation to keep faith with his sovereign and with his fellow subjects.[13]

Of course the duty to seek peace through the civil law has no better standing than does the duty to do so through the natural law.[14] The greater security with which the subject can

---

[11] *Ibid.*, p. 179; see also p. 180; *Leviathan*, p. 234.

[12] TP, II, par. 3; Vaughan, *Studies*, II, 75: "Hobbes could never make up his mind whether expediency suffices as the motive power of man's political and moral life, or whether it needs to be supplemented by the idea of duty. And by way of covering his confusion, he shuffles in the hybrid 'law of nature,' half prudence and half duty, to make a bridge between the two. Of this expedient, Spinoza will have nothing. The 'law of nature' is, to him, merely a convenient phrase for the results yielded by considerations of prudence and expediency. As a law of moral obligation he rejects it root and branch."

[13] Hobbes, *De Cive*, p. 86.

[14] As Warrender repeatedly, and correctly, argues.

obey civil rather than natural law is a legitimate factor in his prudential calculations but cannot in any way introduce "duty" or destroy natural right. It is at this point that we should note Spinoza's principal explicit correction of Hobbes's approach:

With regard to politics, the difference between Hobbes and me, about which you inquire, consists in this that I ever preserve the natural right intact so that the Supreme Power in a State has no more power over a subject than is proportionate to the power by which it is superior to the subject. This is what always takes place in the state of nature.[15]

The individual's right of nature does not cease in the political order. The fact is that man acts in accordance with the laws of his own nature and pursues his own advantage in both the natural and the political order.[16]

Spinoza here makes the assumption that Hobbes's subject has abandoned his natural right upon entering civil society. It is an assumption which is in accord with what Hobbes evidently wishes to say, but which, following his original principles he is unable to say clearly. The nature of man is to seek self-preservation, Hobbes believes, and we must accept this idea as fundamental to his whole thought. In seeking self-preservation, men establish an unlimited sovereign and give up to it both their natural power and their natural right to resist it. The consequences of this moralization of right are systemically disastrous. The sovereign set up to preserve the subject's life may threaten to destroy it.[17] In this extreme case, Hobbes has the choice of going back and revising his definition of the

---

[15] Wolf, *Correspondence*, Ep. 50, p. 269.
[16] TP, III, par. 3.
[17] Locke, *Two Treatises of Government*, p. 372: "This is to think that Men are so foolish that they take care to avoid what Mischiefs may be done them by *Pole-Cats*, or *Foxes*, but are content, nay think it Safety, to be devoured by *Lions*."

nature of man or of denying the loss of natural right in civil society. He does neither; instead he attempts to confine the right of the subject to the single case of the right to resist when the sovereign threatens immediate death. It cannot be so arbitrarily confined even in Hobbes's own writings. At one place, the subject is allowed the reserved right to resist for "bodily protection, free enjoyment of air, water, and all necessaries for life"; at another place, the subject cannot be commanded to execute a parent, and "there are many other cases" in which obedience may be refused; at yet another place, "life and health" may be defended; at last we learn that "every subject retains to himself as much freedom as suffices him to live well and quietly." [18] Such vague and arbitrary limitations will not do. Because Hobbes has previously said firmly that each man has the right to judge of what is necessary to his own preservation, a right which cannot be limited to the state of nature, it follows that it is both right and reasonable for any person or group of persons to resist and actually to overthrow a government which *they* think does or might menace their well-being in any way which *they* consider significant. That this conclusion should follow from Hobbes's own reasonings, and that it should also be the conclusion against which the whole thrust of his writings is directed, is a striking and, apparently, an inescapable finding.

Spinoza avoids this dilemma by denying the relevance of duty, by denying unlimited right to the sovereign, and by retaining the natural right of the subject intact under all conditions—not merely for self-preservation, but for anything at all. Man

has as much right as he has power and strength. It follows that the right and law of nature, under which all men are born and for the most part live, forbids nothing but what nobody desires and nobody can do: it forbids neither strife, nor hatred, nor anger,

[18] Hobbes, *De Cive*, pp. 51, 79, 110, 114.

nor deceit; in short, it is opposed to nothing that appetite can suggest.[19]

Hobbes leans heavily on promises in order to legitimate the duty of the subject to obey the sovereign. Two kinds of promises are involved: voluntary and explicit promises made at the time of the social contract to fellow subjects and to the sovereign; [20] involuntary promises, explicit or not, made to the conqueror in a state founded by force. Hobbes's attempt to show the binding character of promises is not successful. His likening of a broken promise to a logical contradiction, for example, scarcely needs comment. He himself recognizes that fraud involving broken promises is legitimate both between individuals in the state of nature and between independent states. As for the promise made to a conquering sovereign, Hobbes is driven to conclude, for the sake of consistency, that one is also bound to keep a promise extorted by a robber to pay a sum of money "tomorrow" (in the absence of a civil law to the contrary) even though no enforcement of the pledge is possible.[21] It is difficult to see how this can be squared with the later information that our obligation to the sovereign ceases when he is no longer able to afford protection or enforce allegiance. As for the promise made at the social contract, "no one will promise to surrender his right to do everything except with intent to deceive, and no one at all will keep promises save from fear of a greater evil or hope of a greater good." [22] More generally and decisively, from the standpoint of the naturalistic ethics to which both Hobbes and Spinoza are committed, promises can have only the compelling force

[19] TP, II, par. 8.
[20] There is, of course, no contract with the sovereign.
[21] TTP, XVI, 131; Hobbes, De Cive, p. 38; Strauss, p. 234, points out that the obligation to pay the robber is not clear: how much does the loss of money threaten my survival, for instance? Further, what chance is there of the king trusting me if he knows that I will desert him once his power to compel me is gone?
[22] TTP, XVI, 129-31.

which we choose or are forced to accord them; any limitation of right, any system of moral duties or obligations, is irreconcilable with a philosophy which denies freedom of the will and asserts total determinism.[23]

It could probably be shown that most of the debates about Hobbes's meaning derive from his own wavering on the right-equals-power issue.[24] The question of whether Spinoza, holding firmly to that principle, arrives at more coherent results, is in a sense the topic of this study.

Hobbes and Spinoza may appear to agree on the meaning of freedom. Hobbes wrote: "Liberty, that we may define it, is nothing but an absence of the lets and hindrances of motion." [25] Spinoza put it that a man is "free, in so far as he can repel all force, take what vengeance he pleases for harm done him, and, to speak generally, live as his own nature and judgement dicate." [26] Both definitions seem to understand freedom as the absence of external hindrance. We have already spoken of Spinoza's meaning of freedom; it will now be seen as an implicit criticism of that of Hobbes. Both men agree that freedom is greatly limited by the fact that all of a man's actions are determined by preceding states of affairs. Hobbes uses "freedom" in the commonsense way to describe an absence of such obvious restraints as handcuffs, jail walls, policemen. Because he calls the state of nature the state of freedom,[27] he evidently is thinking more of restraints by other men than of natural restraints, such as gravitation and the resistance of natural objects to our will. Least of all does he consider the

---

[23] TP, II, par. 12; TP, III, par. 14. Hobbes, of course, did not believe in free will, but his argument against it is somewhat different from that of Spinoza. Hobbes could not understand determinism as psychic determinism because of his doubt as to the existence of the psyche. See Goldsmith, pp. 26–27.

[24] Plamenatz, I, 80.

[25] Hobbes, *De Cive*, p. 109; *Leviathan*, p. 136.

[26] TP, II, par. 9.

[27] Hobbes, *De Cive*, title of Chapter 1.

difference between what at any given moment I think I want to do and that which I would want to do if I understand my interests and circumstances.[28] Here he must be considered, in comparison with Spinoza, unreflective. That self which is free or not is not the algebraic sum of the present passions accompanied by awareness, nor is a hindrance only an external block—it can also be internal, as in the case of compulsive, irrational, ignorant, or deceived men.[29]

We are here on the shore of a sea of metaphysics, in which I plan to do no more than wade. Does the self exist? Does not a theory of the existence of a self imply a theory of organism; is such a theory defensible? We need not raise these issues here. Hobbes might have taken an extreme behaviorist view of man, but he does not. Man's compulsive drive toward self-preservation, his passions of pride and glorying, of which Hobbes speaks, are self-regarding; they imply an operative unity, more than a synthetic unity of apperception, hardly less than a transcendental ego. If so, then men have a nature, interests which computers do not share, and freedom for them cannot be only the absence of external bonds or blocks, but must also involve sufficient internal control—autonomy—to achieve or work toward purposes dictated by their own structure. Thus Spinoza's statement that freedom is the ability to live according to one's own nature is a coherent statement within the context of an explicitly defined general view, whereas Hobbes's idea of freedom must be taken to be either incoherent or an example of "truncated empiricism." [30]

[28] Santayana, *Dominations and Powers*, p. 422: "Now, by the Will that determines the good proper to any creature, I understand the demands and potentialities of his nature, not of his consciousness."

[29] TP, II, par. 11.

[30] As noted, Hobbes entitled the first part of *De Cive* "Liberty," referring to the freedom of man to express his passionate nature in the state of nature. Significantly, Spinoza calls Part IV of the *Ethics:* "Of Human Bondage, or The Strength of the Emotions." Neither writer, of course, maintains the implied position in its pure form.

Hobbes and Spinoza agree in seeing the state of nature as the ultimate in human degradation, as a condition without law, property, security, or amenity.

Hobbes is much the more interested of the two in the frequent and vivid portrayal of this condition, in showing that the state of nature is implicit in our daily individual precautionary activities and hovers darkly in the background during every political crisis. For him the idea is not only an explanatory device; it is a means to frighten us into accepting his political recommendations. Spinoza uses the state of nature concept to structure a politics of individualism, but if one government falls, the social fabric will endure long enough to form another; his state of nature is at least as horrendous as that of Hobbes but it has less of the aura of historicity, it is not a present threat to us.

Hobbes, as well as Spinoza, deduces the necessities of political life from an understanding of human nature, but much of the difference between their political conclusions arises out of the disparity of their views on what human nature is. For Hobbes, man is much the same in both the civil and the natural states, the same, that is, in being considered simply as a bundle of interests. Hobbes is little interested in the contents of the bundle; he anticipates classical economics, modern group theory, and social Darwinism in analyzing how men get what they want rather than what it is that they want. Hobbes is exhilarated, and so are we, by his savage comparison of the life of man to a race, a struggle with other men for advantage, "with no other goal, nor other garland, but being foremost." [31] The struggle is not merely a life occupation, it is life itself: "to forsake the course, is to die." [32] Hobbes explicitly denies that there is a good for man, a good other than the satisfaction of this passion and then of that and then of another.[33] He and

---

[31] Hobbes, *English Works*, IV, 52–53.
[32] *Ibid.*, p. 53.
[33] Hobbes, *Leviathan*, p. 63; *De Cive*, pp. 29, 166.

Spinoza do not differ in viewing man as motivated solely by self-serving desires; they differ in that Hobbes believes the egoism always takes the form of competition with other men, whereas Spinoza does not.[34]

Hobbes's civil society might be understood as an attempt to institutionalize the struggle, as a truly British attempt to enforce fair play, to the end that the contestants may be more comfortable, less bloody, and better equipped to display their talents, so that fouls and low behavior may be lessened. For him, the peace of civil society is the war of nature carried on by other means. For Spinoza, the nature of man is not competitive but self-preserving, self-realizing, and this is best achieved initially by moderating the conditions of competition and then by working toward that cooperation between men which is necessary to the purposes of each man.

The difference is fundamental. Here again, Spinoza's position is a criticism of that of Hobbes. The end of man cannot simultaneously be self-preservation and competitive advantage over other men unless the means of preservation are in such short supply that victory over other men is identical with survival. Hobbes does not assert this; [35] victory in the race may as a by-product enhance one's survival potentialities, but the essence of success is the joy in having outstripped a competitor. Spinoza maintains Hobbes's original self-preservation thesis and keeps the analysis of the passions tied to it at all times. Self-realization is not an addition to self-preservation but a development out of it.

Not only does Hobbes, in his study of the passions, forget his original postulation of the primacy of the drive for self-preservation, he also fails adequately to account either for the

---

[34] TTP, III, 51; TTP, V, 93; at E, IV, prop. 68, Spinoza recognizes that men are actually very competitive at the level of passion: "Each combatant is seized with a fierce desire to put down his rivals in every possible way, till he who at last comes out victorious is more proud of having done harm to others than of having done good to himself."

[35] He almost does, at *Leviathan*, p. 64.

conflict of passions or for their source. Worse, he compromises what consistency his view of man as competitive might have by turning from theory to observation and speaking of "curiosity," [36] and the "glorying man." [37]

Hobbes and Spinoza are both political egalitarians, but Hobbes is also a psychological "Leveler," in the sense that he denies the possibility of significant individual differences among men. Even prudence, "equal time, equally bestows on all men," [38] and wisdom is the result of experience only. [39]

Both Hobbes and Spinoza were charged with teaching faithlessness and immorality. The charge is false as applied to the intent of either, but in the case of Hobbes, some unforeseen theoretical consequences of his system amount to just that, at least as his contemporaries would have understood it. The survival of society or the civil state requires a readiness on the part of its members to perform actions which are not, for them, self-preserving in the immediate, Hobbesian, sense of physical survival. Hobbes offers no rationale for such actions; there is reason to think that he felt that a sensible man would not undertake them. In the case of military service of a distinctly hazardous character, he was no doubt correct in assuming that every society contains a sufficient number of unreflective daredevils who may be hired by the state (or as substitutes by individuals) to defend it against other, foreign or domestic, daredevils. Hobbes, born to natural fear and matured to rational caution, would have thought them all fools. No doubt many of them are, but it is an odd political position which trusts that our side will have more, or bigger, fools than the other, and which implies that even we must submit to have that name applied to us should we ever happen

[36] Hobbes, *Leviathan*, p. 35.
[37] Goldsmith, pp. 79–82, 244–45.
[38] Hobbes, *Leviathan*, p. 80.
[39] Hobbes, *De Cive*, p. 2. The influence of Bacon's naive empiricism is here evident.

to hazard our persons for a cause other than immediate personal safety.

Hobbes and Spinoza view the state as an artificial arrangement for the betterment of the lot of individual men and they agree that it cannot be too powerful if it is to achieve that end. Using an argument which he admits may not be conclusive, Hobbes defends unlimited monarchy as the best form of sovereignty. Possibly the national emergency in which he wrote and his desire for immediate and conclusive peace hurried him into a premature synthesis. Spinoza looks farther ahead. Hobbes may be understood to have written for Cromwell and the Stuarts; Spinoza looked ahead to 1688.

The natural harmony of interests which Hobbes assumes to exist in the civil society between citizen and sovereign, and between citizen and citizen as regards the maintenance of the sovereign, is not credible, and is the less so when we recall the savagery of the competition previously postulated. Spinoza reminds us that power corrupts,[40] that stupidity is often enthroned, that the interests of the monarch are often understood by the monarch himself to consist in keeping his subjects poor, weak, and divided.[41] The monarch is most likely to seek glory in international affairs, waging wars for new territory, for vanity, for the interests of his foreign relatives. Seldom will these wars be in the interest of the subjects, usually they will lead to the impoverishment of all. The stability which Hobbes hoped to find in unlimited monarchy will not be found there.

Hobbes and Spinoza agree in favoring absolute sovereignty, but Hobbes's identification of absolute government with arbitrary government is mistaken. As we have said, the most absolute government is not the most arbitrary government but

[40] TP, VI, par. 3.
[41] TP, V, par. 7; TP, VIII, par. 31; Aristotle *Politics* 1313b; Rousseau, *Social Contract*, Bk. III, Ch. 6, p. 70.

the least; the most absolute government is that in which subjects participate to the greatest extent. Arbitrary government
cannot command the enthusiastic support of subjects and
therefore is less absolute, weaker against foreign attack or
revolution; [42] if it survives against external foes, it is because
they are in no better condition; if it escapes revolution, it does
so only by weakening those subjects who are its only strength;
its peace is the peace of the grave. [43]

Hobbes urges his unlimited monarchy upon us as the best
form of the state. Spinoza is more than doubtful about the
value of the solution Hobbes proposes and is not at all inclined
to accept a political settlement which so abruptly cuts short
the possibilities of man's future development. A good state, he
thinks, is not one of a predetermined form, but one which
matches the condition of its members, which encourages, or at
least allows, their progress to rationality, and which is itself
sufficiently flexible to permit of improvement when possible.
Hobbes's sovereign is acceptable only as a hero-founder, to
create the society which will render him superfluous.

In his defense of unlimited monarchy, Hobbes argues
against the possibility of constitutional governments: [44]

If it were possible there could be such a state, it would no whit
advantage the liberty of the subject. For as long as they all agree,
each single citizen is as much a subject as possibly he can be: but
if they disagree, the state returns to a civil war. [45]

Spinoza's difference here from Hobbes's abstract deduction is
based on understanding of political probability, and in this
area proof is not easily had. [46] However, the history of English
government was soon to exemplify Hobbes's "impossible

---

[42] TP, VII, par. 14.
[43] TP, VI, par. 4.
[44] Hobbes accepts a degree of constitutionalism in *De Cive*, p. 125.
[45] *Ibid.*, p. 89.
[46] TTP, XVII, 163. Spinoza too had his doubts about constitutional
monarchy: TTP, XVII, 187–89.

state." [47] as the course of Greek history took the meaning out of Aristotle's definition of man as a city-state animal.

Hobbes probably, and Spinoza clearly, were profoundly influenced by Machiavelli, but only Spinoza followed him in the importance he attributed to the character of the people, in his concept of a national character. It was necessary to Hobbes, if he were to arrive convincingly at his desired conclusion, that the masses never—except fleetingly at the foundation of the civil order—be regarded as anything but a dispersed multitude, an aggregate of, rather than a system of, individuals.[48] This outlook was necessary to him in order that any slightest disturbance of the civil order might be seen to present a threat of the return to the state of nature, and that his concept of sovereignty might be exhibited in all its stark necessity and without the distracting background of mediating institutions or an independently existing society.

Machiavelli and Spinoza met the problem of the appearance of a social structure, apparently out of nowhere, with a theory of hero-founders. Hero-founders do more than found regimes; they found a people, a society with intense internal cohesive forces displayed in an infinitely ramified reticulation of customs, relationships, and commonly held values. Hobbes was right in believing that society could not long survive without government, but he greatly reduced the value of his theory by assuming that society could not survive the particular government which it had at some particular moment, in not considering that a society might have the capacity to dismantle one government and frame another.

If subjects could not change governments without reverting to the state of nature, then there could remain no right of revolution, not even "by the consent of all the subjects to-

---

[47] Pollock, *Chronicum Spinozarum*, p. 57: "Modern constitutional politics begin with the English Revolution of 1688. Spinoza's conceptions of political mechanism belong to an ancient world. Nevertheless the objects he sought to attain were much like those of the English parliamentary leaders."

[48] Hobbes, *De Cive*, p. 135.

gether." [49] Hobbes did his best to destroy every possible justification for resistance to the sovereign, and thus removed the
only real limitation on despotism and stagnation.

Spinoza also sees man as a bundle of interests, but of interests broader and yet more structured than those which
Hobbes discusses. Spinoza does not see the need for subordi-
nating every interest to the single interest in political stability. If government is an artificial institution for the forwarding of men's interests, then it must forward them, as much and
as many of them as possible. This is best done by allowing
them actual expression in the arena of society and of political
action, even though such freedom may result in the threat or
reality of revolt.

"Actual expression" implies freedom of speech; Hobbes
will have none of it:

> It very much concerns the interest of peace, that no opinions or
> doctrines be delivered to citizens, by which they may imagine,
> that either by right they may not obey the laws of the city . . .
> or that it is lawful to resist him.[50]

Later, he says of the sovereign, "that he both judge what
opinions and doctrines are enemies unto peace and also that he
forbid them to be taught," [51] and, the sovereign is to root
"certain perverse doctrines" out of the minds of men.

Hobbes's position is not indefensible. Even for Spinoza,
who advocated freedom of speech,[52] a nation in an extreme
situation not only may but should do whatever is necessary
for self-preservation. Hobbes's England was threatened, in the
year of his birth, with an invasion which some English Catholics were thought to support; in his maturity he saw the public
peace senselessly, as he thought, broken by religious contro-

---

[49] *Ibid.*, p. 85.
[50] Hobbes, *De Cive*, p. 75.
[51] *Ibid.*, p. 76.
[52] TTP (Dover), Pref., pp. 5, 6, 11; TTP, XVIII, 199; TTP (Dover),
XIII, 180–81; TTP, XIV, 123.

versy. Yet a political view framed for extreme situations can hardly be generally satisfactory; Hobbes goes too far in saying: "But private men, while they assume to themselves the knowledge of good and evil, desire to be even as kings, which cannot be with the safety of the commonweal." [53]

Spinoza thought that the suppression of free speech would entail the suppression of thought itself and the defeat of man's struggle to realize his essential need to understand, and, further, that in diminishing the power of the subject it weakened the state power it meant to support:

Seeing that we have the rare happiness of living in a republic, where everyone's judgement is free and unshackled, and where each may worship God as his conscience dictates, and where freedom is esteemed before all things dear and precious, I have believed that I should be undertaking no ungrateful or unprofitable task, in demonstrating that not only can such freedom be granted without prejudice to the public peace, but also, that without such freedom, piety cannot flourish, nor the public peace be secure.

Such is the chief conclusion I seek to establish in this treatise . . .[54]

Spinoza, too, saw his country beset by frantic preachers and the actual head of state, Jan DeWitt, whom he ardently supported, murdered by a mob incited by those same preachers. Yet he argued for freedom even to speak against the laws, provided that the laws were in the meantime obeyed.[55] His belief that freedom of speech should be allowed was based not on any notion of right but on the pragmatic judgment that the interests of both nation and citizen were thus advanced.[56]

There is an interesting, though minor, theoretical problem in Hobbes's position that might be mentioned. When he allows that a nation's laws cannot be unjust, though they may

[53] Hobbes, *De Cive*, p. 129.
[54] TTP (Dover), Pref., p. 6.
[55] *Ibid.*; TP, VIII, par. 46; TTP, XX, 231.
[56] TTP, XX, 235, 239, 241, 243; TP, VII, par. 5.

be pernicious, who, in the actual case, can make the judgment that they are indeed pernicious? Hobbes himself has "avoided coming ashore" [57] and is not writing as a citizen of any particular country but as a disembodied intellect—or rather as one who is philosophically in a state of nature with every government and therefore is free to make criticisms of all. But could an actual citizen be permitted, by Hobbes's standards, to notice, even within the privacy of his own mind, that a law was pernicious? Since it can hardly be denied that he must on occasion notice such a fact, is he not at that moment in revolt?

Hobbes's writings contain no reference to Spinoza— Hobbes had completed all his major works before Spinoza's name was known—but he did make one remark that has been recorded; it was that "he durst not write so boldly." [58] There is hardly any doubt that Hobbes was referring to Spinoza's writings on religion and implying, further, that he would have expressed similar opinions had he dared. Briefly, Spinoza's writings denied the truth of revealed religions, denied that any such religion *could* be true, and denied that religion was even directed toward truth. We may assume that Hobbes agreed.

As for freedom of religion, however, which Spinoza's theory allows and which Hobbes's does not, the latter is once more driven by the conflicting forces of logic and the fear of public opinion into confusion. Princes must sin

against the law of nature, if they cause not such a doctrine to be taught and practiced (or permit a contrary to be taught and practiced) as they believe necessarily conduceth to the eternal salvation of their subjects. [59]

This Erastian doctrine that the only belief to be tolerated is the belief held by the sovereign comes very close to the conclusion that there is no intrinsic truth in religious beliefs at all. This was unsayable in Hobbes's time and country; his

[57] Hobbes, *De Cive*, p. 6.
[58] Aubrey, I, 357; Feuer, pp. 276–77.
[59] Hobbes, *De Cive*, p. 143.

attempt to reconcile his political conclusions with a specious display of respect for the truth of religion leads him into endless ambiguities. He can be brought back to theoretical consistency only if we decide to regard as merely tactful all of his statements which imply the existence of an objective religious truth. We cannot, however, discern much political sagacity in his opinion that the political troubles of seventeenth-century England would be eased if all religious beliefs but those of a state church were outlawed. Admittedly, the situation in his country was very difficult, but he had the example of the Netherlands before him to show that religious toleration was not incompatible with the mobilization of sufficient national unity to enable a tiny country to defeat religiously monolithic Spain. The details of Spinoza's treatment of religion will be set forth in a later chapter.

To summarize: it is impossible to improve on Spinoza's own statement of the difference between his own and Hobbes's political theories; it lay in Spinoza's holding fast to the principle of inalienable natural right and its equivalence to natural power. The differences at the metaphysical level are more numerous and complex; principal among them, perhaps, are their opposite views on the ontological status of the world of thought, on the relation of reason to fact, and on the role of ethics.[60]

There is no intention in the above criticisms of Hobbes to belittle him as a political philosopher. Without Hobbes there could have been, as far as political thought goes, no Spinoza. Spinoza saw farther, it is here maintained, but only because he stood on Hobbes's shoulders—and Hobbes stood very high. What *is* intended is a clarification of Spinoza's views and the making of the point that much of the controversy that rages over what Hobbes and Hobbism means could be brought closer to settlement if we consulted his greatest contemporary and subtlest commentator.

[60] Zac, p. 237; Janet, II, 259–60.

X

Obligation

❖

IT HAS been said that the question of obligation is a central problem of political philosophy,[1] meaning, perhaps, that in a particular thinker's treatment of obligation we will find the key to his whole thought.

On the other hand, such men as Plato, Aristotle, Marx, and others showed no great interest in the matter of obligation. Perhaps the question "what is the state?" is the real core of every political outlook. Even such condensed formulations as: "*l'état c'est moi,*" "how does the state differ from a band of robbers?" "man is a city-state animal," and "the state is the executive committee of the ruling class," may be taken to be miniature political philosophies in themselves. One of the most important questions we can ask about the character of the state, however, is: How is it related to the individual and the individual to it? Which is the fundamental entity, the state or the person? Who dreams whom?

These are the same questions asked by the analyst of political obligation, although for him they appear in the form: "Why should I obey the law?" It does not matter, then, whether we consider the character of the state or the nature of political obligation to be paramount; by either route we arrive at the same questions.

The matter of political obligation was particularly crucial in the early and late parts of the period between St. Paul and

[1] Berlin, pp. 7, 33; d'Entreves, "Obeying Whom," pp. 1–14.

Hegel. This is not the place to ask why this was so, although some historical connection with a widespread and basic division of loyalties seems evident. Before St. Paul, the question was dormant; since the British Hegelians it has been shelved, at least to the extent that the alternatives between radical individualism and organic or holistic views are clearly set forth: one is basically a Humean or an Hegelian,[2] the rest is individual variation.

Within the late part of the period mentioned, but especially in the seventeenth century, the problem of political obligation was central for every major thinker (with the exception of Machiavelli). A principal reason for the general depreciation of Locke, as a political theorist, is the fact that he founded his theory of political obligation on promises and on the rights of man, which is to say that he evaded the issue. Hobbes, as we have seen, met the issue squarely, in principle, only to lose his answer in ambiguities.

It was suggested above that there are but two possible general theories of the state, and of our obligation to obey it, now available: the organic and the individualist. We need not consider the relative merits of the two approaches, although the thought is put forward, without argument, that Spinoza might have to some extent bridged the gap between them; he has been thought, by different commentators, to have been a precursor of the philosophy of organism and also as among the first of the radical individualists.

In the English-speaking world, political thinkers with a leaning toward an organic view of the state have had the most difficulty in framing a plausible theory of obligation. If my very being and most intimate thought are social products, if society itself, in its institutions and climates of opinion, is completely adaptive, functional, then several things follow: First, talk of my duty to the state is less serious, because I am less serious; I do not exist in the same full sense in which

[2] There is a third option—the Kantian—which has almost no adherents.

society exists. I may be more subtly tied to my culture than the ant is to his heap, but the tie is as strong; for me to pretend to analyze my culture objectively, to categorize its manifestations in abstract terms, to attempt to think of it as though I were not part of it, is to be subject to a harmless illusion, to be mentally ill, or even to be dangerous, depending upon whether I exemplify a socially useful attitude such as the "Protestant ethic," form part of an *avant garde* fighting for adjustive social change, or drift into alienated deliquency. In any case, whether I am an inspired innovator or a subway sadist, my actions are socially caused; to talk to me of my obligations may affect my social behavior—but can I have any obligations? Second, although it is in some intuitive sense clear that the cells of my body are subordinate to and have a kind of "duty" to my whole person, it has not yet proven possible to set forth this alleged fact in discursive form and without reliance on analogy. Third, he who tells us that the state is an animal has told us little unless he goes on to tell us what kind of animal it is and what it requires of us, its subordinate parts. No consensus on this matter can be found among the members of the organic school; if it could be found, we should be entitled to ask how they who hold it have exempted themselves from the subjectivity they ascribe to others. This epistemological question is, for organic state theorists, perhaps the most difficult of all.

The individualist view can be taken for granted. Insofar as it relates to Spinoza's view of political obligation, it is presented below. In any case, with the significant exception of our sociologists, it has been the uncriticized assumption of the English-speaking world for some time. Also, individualist thinkers have been rather casual about their principles of political obligation, basing them at times with Spinoza on self-interest, at other times on natural law, on religion, on contract, on common sense, or on whatever comes to hand.

By the seventeenth century, the uncritical acceptance of the role of king and priest, of hierarchy on earth and in heaven, of the theory of a single Christendom, and of the rule of custom and authority, had come to an end. Not completely, of course, or for all, but thinking people, and some who were not, knew that they lived in a new world in which many of the old oughts and musts had lost their peremptory character. Religious reformers and zealots, commercial interests, national monarchs, and natural philosophers disrupted respectively the religious, economic, feudal, and cosmological orders. Group solidarities relaxed; the single person became the unit to be dealt with, and men felt distanced from other men. In the Italian renaissance, the resulting individualism might have been welcomed as a liberation; later, and in the northern parts of Europe, it was soberly accepted as a fact and a problem of life.

The political problem was the legitimation of a secular political order.[3] It was a larger problem than it might at first appear. An institution requires for legitimacy not only the arousal of the feeling that it fits in with the past, as a familiar object in the landscape, but also the acceptance of the thought that it fits in with the prevailing conception of what is metaphysically real and valuable. Because no one such conception did prevail, it became necessary for political thinkers to be persuasive metaphysicians.

The religious question was everywhere in the forefront. Even to the casual glance, the situation was extraordinarily complex. In France, a Catholic king and people were ranged against a strong Protestant minority; in England, kings nominally Protestant but with actual Catholic leanings were supported by conservative Protestants against a wide range of Calvinist and Anabaptist sects; in the United Provinces, a largely Protestant war against the Catholic king of Spain

---

[3] Really a double problem: politics had to be secularized first, and then legitimated; TTP, XVII, 157. Even Hobbes did not believe in the divine right of kings; he believed in kings.

had ended in national liberation and the consequent confrontation of a small, religiously liberal, ruling class by a mass of
doctrinaire Calvinists who supported the claim of a pretender
to a throne which had never quite existed. Scattered throughout these countries, as well as in Germany, were small groups
of inspired radical dissenters who were religious, and therefore
political, anarchists.

The political arguments centered about such topics as the
contract between king and people, the divine or other right of
kings to rule and to determine religious practice, the inherent
natural right of men to religious and political self-
determination, and the will of God in all these questions. The
arguments—did the opponents listen to each other long
enough to justify calling them debates?—ranged through the
Old and New Testaments, in both of which it is clearly
shown that subjects must and must not resist temporal authority, that faith and works, or perhaps only one of them, were
necessary for salvation, that reason, or authority, or tradition,
or conscience was the sole safe guide to action.

The tacit acceptance of individualism involved also the
consequence that the individual must judge of what is true,
and every important thinker of the time accepted this conclusion, although some maintained that the judgment was not by
right, or that it ought not be exercised. Correctly so, it might
seem. If each man were granted the right to interpret Scripture, there would arise as many Scriptures and Popes to interpret them as there were men who cared to exercise the right,
each of them qualified to direct kings and other men on the
inexpugnable basis of the word of God. This meant the end of
government, of order, of society.

Beside the authority of Scripture stood the authority of the
natural law. But, as the seventeenth century suspected, and the
eighteenth century was to experience, natural law is no support for the defenders of law and order. Scripture was an
arsenal of arguments both for and against the power of the

state over the individual; natural law was not only subject to the same capriciousness of individual interpretation but, in its ancient original sources, supported reason against statute law, spoke of the rights of subjects against sovereigns, dallied with justifications of tyrannicide. Natural law had further been somewhat compromised by its long association with and partial assimilation to canon law. Machiavelli had long ago discarded it completely.

What arguments, then, were available to those who saw the secular state as desirable or necessary and wanted to show that it should be supported? More particularly, why should I obey the law?

What is obligation? A man has lent me a sum of money which is to be repaid on a certain day. The day come, I stand money in hand beside him before the judge. I refuse to pay. The judge says, "You are obliged to pay." "How am I obliged?" I reply. He says:

"You are morally obliged to pay because God has commanded in his book that you not covet your neighbors' goods. As an acknowledged authority, I certify that the Scriptures are indeed the word of God and that this command applies in your case. Aside from the Scriptures, as an acknowledged prophet, I tell you that God has revealed to me, and accompanied the relevation with miracles, that you are obliged to pay this debt. I remind you further that God has implanted his divine law in your own mind and that it tells you that in this case you must pay.

"You are morally obliged to obey the commands of the state; the law of the state is that you must pay and I, the representative of the state, command you to do so. Your obligation to the state arises out of your contract, both explicit and implicit, to obey it; out of your duty to obey lawful rulers as set forth in the Bible; out of the character of the state as God's representative on earth; and out of gratitude for benefits received from the state.

"Your moral obligation to obey God arises out of the fact that he has created you, that he has command over your destiny in the present as well as in the future life, that your nature is to love and obey him, and that he is infinitely stronger than you.

"Moral obligation also arises out of the law of nature, which I tell you, commands the repayment of debts both by reason of equity and gratitude and by reason of its definition of justice, which is that we should render to each what is his own. The law of nature is known to you by my interpretation, by the consensus of all men, by the authority of leading writers, and by the light of your own reason.

"You are further morally obliged to pay on the basis of your own promise, freely given, to break which is obviously immoral. Further, to break a promise is to commit a kind of insane act, to contradict yourself by saying, and saying not, at once.

"Finally, your culture defines morality as paying in these circumstances and you are bound by the moral judgment of the society in which you live.

"You are prudentially bound to pay because if you do not you risk present imprisonment and future damnation. No one will lend you money again, no matter what your need; people who owe you money now or in the future will not repay you; your standing in the community and your whole career, as well as your own self-esteem, will suffer.

"You are prudentially obliged to pay because, if you do not, the social fabric of trust on which all, including you yourself, rely, will be weakened, as will also the state on which you depend for your defense.

"To put the matter as clearly as possible, you are prudentially obliged because I put this pistol to your head and say, and you know truly, that I will kill you at this moment if you do not pay.

"You are physically obliged because I and these other men

grasp you firmly, direct your hand with the money toward your creditor, and pry your fingers open. This failing, we hypnotize you, drug you, so that you pay or not at our will, not knowing what you do.

"More subtly, we know that your rationality is so firm that you will not be able to resist our prudential arguments, your fear of God is such that you will be frightened or awed into paying, and we have in our society so raised and conditioned you that your shame at not paying will certainly overmaster all other considerations."

"Moral," "prudential," "physical": these categories of obligation tend to merge under analysis; it may frequently be impossible to say which applies in a given situation, yet there seems no better way to discriminate among types of obligation.

For some, the whole meaning of obligation lies in the moral ought and should. Spinoza rejects the possibility of moral obligation. His reply to the above complex statement, though not in the same order, would run as follows:

"The Bible says that I shall not covet my neighbor's goods, but it also, in the Old Testament, provides for a regular cancellation of debts. According to the New Testament, Christ himself drove the moneylenders out of the temple and said we should forgive our debtors. Therefore, the Scripture contradicts itself and thus says nothing,[4] or else it requires an interpretation. But neither Pope nor prophet can claim to have the exclusive right to interpret Scripture, because such a right must arise out of Scripture itself or be confirmed by miracles.[5] Scripture itself, however, does not name any present interpreters of its message;[6] as for miracles, Scripture itself tells us of false miracles and lying prophets. There are, in fact, no miracles. The evidence for them is poor, and they contradict

[4] TTP (Dover), II, 40; TTP, XI, 163.
[5] TTP (Dover), VII, 107, 119.
[6] TTP (Dover), VII, 118; TTP (Dover), XV, 198.

the nature of God in that his existence is shown by the regularities of nature and disproven by what seem to be its discontinuities.[7] In any case, the prophets knew only what was suggested to them by their imagination; the entire Old Testament was meant only for the ancient Hebrews, to teach them obedience. It has no present relevance.[8] The New Testament offers a counsel of perfection only; it issues no commands. The text, but not the message, of both testaments is obscure, incomplete, and corrupt [9] and there is no reason to think that they are divinely inspired in any special sense. Scripture is, in fact, quite useless to rational men.[10] The divine law which is innately in the minds of all men is the law of reason; it is therefore not a law at all but a counsel, unless we consider it as the set of unbreakable laws of nature.[11] Finally, there is no God in the sense of a king who issues commands and creates obligations. The 'commands' of God are the order of nature or nature itself; they create no obligation; they cannot be disobeyed.[12]

"As for the state, there are no moral elements in my obligation to obey it.[13] I do so only to the extent to which my rational calculations show that it is to my interest. I hope no more than that the same rational self-interest will guide the state in its treatment of me, in full confidence that if we are both sufficiently intelligent in our understanding of our own real interest, each of us will be content with the other. Gratitude and promises create no moral obligation to the state or to persons, for although I recognize that it is usually better to keep promises and to be grateful, possibly even at the cost of

[7] TTP (Dover), Pref., p. 9; TTP (Dover), I, 25; TTP (Dover), VI, 87, 97, 100; TTP (Dover), II, 28–29.

[8] TTP (Dover), Pref., p. 8; TTP (Dover), I, 4, 25; TTP, III, 59.

[9] TTP (Dover), XI, 158; TTP (Dover), XII, 172; TTP (Dover), VII, 98, 108–13; TTP (Dover), X, 151.

[10] TTP, V, 103; TTP (Dover), VII, 100.

[11] TTP (Dover), Pref., p. 9; TTP, XIX, 207; TTP (Dover), I, 25.

[12] TTP, IV, 79; TTP, III, 53.

[13] TTP, XVI, 141.

one's life, I do not see what is added to that interest by calling it moral.

"As for the law of nature, in the classical and medieval sense, what is that but another name for the prejudices of him who cites it? The thought that nature intends a regularity is a vulgar error. The dictate of reason, mentioned above in connection with the divine law, is not a command but a statement of probable actual or logical consequences which may suggest a certain course of action or thought and even, if we are exceptionally rational, compel it, but it cannot create a moral obligation. The consensus of men, or of authorities, is a fiction,[14] but fiction or not, it can create no obligation for me.

"My promise does not bind me morally. I gave it in order to secure my advantage; I may break it for the same purpose.[15] If you say it would not be to my interest to break it, you are no longer talking to me of moral obligation.

"The moral judgments of my society might, when effectively internalized, create in me a sense of moral obligation beyond which I could not appeal, did I not have access to an objective order of thought which is not culturally determined.[16] Because I do have such access, I can see that my society has no command over my moral nature;[17] I can see that the moral judgments of my society are the confused statements of passionate men. Its moral pronouncements usually refer to such things as money, reputation, and pleasure, to such things as can hardly concern a serious man; in their more ethereal guise, they are mere formulas for use in church and on solemn occasions; they have no relevance to the ordinary life of anyone.

"As for physical obligation, I acknowledge that your physical power to compel or deceive me into paying gives you the

---

[14] But see TTP, IV, 81.

[15] TTP, XVI, 131; TP, II, par. 12; TP, III, par. 14; TP, IV, par. 6.

[16] TTP (Dover), I, 14; TTP, IV, 73–75.

[17] TTP (Dover), Pref., p. 10: "No one is bound to live as another pleases."

right to do so, though the question of whether it is better for you to do so in the light of your own long-term interests remains to be investigated. Besides, there is no point in discussing your ability to compel me—you need only do it.

"Only prudential obligation remains as a basis on which our minds may meet. Let me say at once that I am convinced by your prudential arguments, and I now discharge my debt. I do so, however, after a calculation which excludes some of the factors you have mentioned; I have valued some of the considerations you brought forward differently from the way you do, and I have taken into account matters which you have not mentioned. For, let me observe, I am prudentially obliged only to do those things which appeal to my own sense of prudence, not yours,[18] except to the extent to which I judge it prudent to take your advice in the absence of a firm opinion of my own. Also, to say that I am prudentially bound by my own opinion of what is advantageous for me is the same as to say that I am physically bound, for I cannot do other than that which at each moment seems best for me. Thus, you see, I cast out prudential as well as moral obligation, with this difference, that moral obligation, although useful in discourse to the ignorant and passionate multitude, should have no place in the thought of rational men, whereas prudential obligation is quite suitable for ordinary intelligent discussion as long as we bear in mind that in an ultimate sense all obligation is of the physical sort—that is, that we are creatures all of whose actions and thoughts are completely determined, either from within or from without."

Spinoza does not advocate disloyalty, ingratitude, or the breaking of promises and treaties.[19] Machiavelli may give the impression that in a corrupt society the good man, doomed to a life of frustration and defeat, may appropriately display his

---

[18] TTP, XVI, 129, 131, 143.

[19] TTP, XX, 233; TP, III, pars. 17, 18; E, IV, prop. 18; TTP, XVI, 131. Rational men in a reasonable society will keep faith.

virtue by a contemptuous disregard for the decencies; it is hardly possible to misunderstand Spinoza in this way. It is always clear that for him the more intelligent man is the more upright man, the one least under the control of the unenlightened passions, the one least likely to make those shortsighted calculations of his own advantage which bring harm to others. Spinoza's statements are sometimes shocking, as when he says simply that promises need not be kept,[20] but we must understand such sayings in the context of his complete thought.[21] That thought is utilitarian and egocentric, but it is not the narrow utility and selfishness of immediate ends unimaginatively envisioned but the utility of the whole life of a man whose goal is understanding and "the intellectual love of God."

The terms "right" and "wrong" serve no good purpose in the study of politics. No matter what is said to or by him, each man will and must follow his own interest.[22] To say that men ought not to do this, or to set forth utopias in which they do not, is to lose oneself in "obvious fantasies"[23] and to involve political man in a morass of guilt, hypocrisy, self-deception, and recrimination. Yet, if altruism is unattainable, a heightened intelligence is not. If we must find fault with men, we would do well to do so not because they are selfish but because they are stupidly so, because, sunk in crude passion, they deny themselves their own advantage and find themselves in opposition to other men.

Nowhere else do we find the principle of utility expressed with the logical precision and breadth of outlook which Spinoza brought to it. A weakness of the utilitarian tradition has been its view of man in society as engaged in a partnership with other men involving matters peripheral to his real inter-

[20] TTP, XVI, 131–33; TP, II, par. 12.
[21] E, IV, prop. 72; E, V, prop. 38.
[22] TTP, XVII, 179: "the motive of self-interest, which is the strength and life of all human actions."
[23] TP, I, par. 1.

ests. It may be less necessary than once to assail the concept of man as an economic animal, but it is presently appropriate to object to the idea of man as an interest-bearing animal whose interests are of the sort that can be understood by circulating a questionnaire.

The history of utilitarianism, and of the empiricisms which followed it, can be seen in the light of Spinoza's thought to have been the history of the trivialization of philosophy; from Hobbes to Dewey, empiricist utilitarianism, seeking its justification in practicality and public acceptance, has come to the unintended conclusion that the man who refuses "by breaking faith to free himself from the danger of present death" is a fool. Without going through Spinoza's argument that the man may not be a fool, we may notice that philosophy as a human enterprise must adjust to some basic human outlooks or fail. If philosophy is to be the finding of bad reasons for good actions, so much the worse for it, but reasons it must find, for its ultimate criterion may be that it justify to men that which they know in themselves to be beyond the elementary arithmetic of utility. We have long since learned to smile at the pretensions of ethical philosophers, such as Spinoza, that they have been driven by logic or experience to their conclusions; we may be forgiven a like geniality toward recent social scientists who "discover" that personal autonomy is a goal for man, or that integration of personality is the objective meaning of mental stability. Reisman's autonomous man and Erikson's integrated personality [24] are the same men we have met as Spinoza's exemplar, as the Socratic ideal of the classics, as the man of Simonides.[25]

As for Spinoza, his idea that rational men will naturally be mutually accommodating can be taken at the level of narrow self-interest, "one hand washing the other," and of course it is

[24] Erikson, pp. 240, 268, 415.
[25] Plato *Protagoras* 339a; Aristotle *Nicomachean Ethics* 1100b.

also true there.[26] What he is more interested in telling us is that not all men, but rational men, are indeed political animals who, by the necessities of their understanding, will sacrifice everything but their very being for their fellow men. That very being cannot be sacrificed, for it is the integrity of a wholly sane intelligence, the essence and the reward of virtue, in the light of which the fear of personal extinction vanishes.[27]

So much for the principle of obligation. What about the practice? Man's obligation to the state is best described as prudential—but what are his prudentially conceived duties? They are considerable:

There is no doubt that devotion to country is the highest form of piety a man can show, for once the state is destroyed nothing good can survive, but everything is put to hazard; anger and wickedness rule unchallenged and terror fills every heart. It follows that any act of piety towards a neighbor would become an act of impiety if it caused harm to the state as a whole; while any act of impiety towards him would be reckoned as piety if it were done for the state's preservation. For instance, when someone is at odds with me and wants to take my coat, it is a pious act to give him my cloak as well; but once it is decided that this is harmful to the state's preservation, it then becomes pious to summon him to court, even though he must be condemned to death.[28]

This is exactly how Augustine and Luther interpreted the political reference of the Christian ethic of perfection.[29] Here, too, as elsewhere, Spinoza speaks of a threatened return to the state of nature in a way more reminiscent of Hobbes than indicative of his own political intent.[30]

---

[26] E, IV, prop. 71.
[27] E, V, prop. 38; E, IV, prop. 72.
[28] TTP, XIX, 211–13; see also TTP (Dover), VII, 105–106; TP, III, par. 10; E, IV, prop. 63.
[29] Augustine *City of God* xix. 16–21; Deane, pp. 142, 163–66; Luther, p. 375.
[30] TTP, XVIII, 199; TTP, XIX, 205, 213.

There is also some ambiguity in Spinoza's description of what it is to which the citizen's loyalty is to be attached. In the above passage it is one's country (*patriam*); a little later, "the people's welfare is the highest law";[31] elsewhere it is the state, the sovereign, or society. More will be said of this matter in the next chapter, but we may take it that Spinoza always means the welfare of the people as a whole to be taken as the ultimate object of loyalty; where he uses other terms he is thinking of normal times in which the will of the sovereign can in general be taken to be directed toward that welfare.[32]

Some passages in Spinoza's original text, or in the translations, might suggest an interpretation of his meaning of obligation different from that made above: "The sovereign is bound by no law . . . all citizens must [*debere*] obey it in all things, since they have contracted to do so, either tacitly or expressly."[33]

It is clear, however, in context, that the obligation arises out of the contract not because contracts themselves create obligation, but because by their contract the subjects have put themselves in the physical power of the sovereign.

We are bound [*exequi tenemur*] to perform all the commands of the sovereign without exception; for no matter how foolish they may be, reason still bids us perform them so as to choose the lesser evil.[34]

This statement is incomplete in that it disregards those who are not reasonable men, except insofar as even they can see the physical dangers of breaking the laws, but as it stands it still points only to prudential obligation.

Everyone will be bound [*parere tenebitur*] to obey it either in freedom of spirit or from fear of the supreme penalty.[35]

[31] TTP, XIX, 213.
[32] TTP, XVI, 133; note also TP, VII, par. 12.
[33] TTP, XVI, 133.
[34] *Ibid.*
[35] *Ibid*

This is more adequate in that it takes into account two extremes within the population—philosophers and men subject only to force. Spinoza does not here account for the type of obligation relevant to men of the middle mass of subjects; possibly because of the difficulty in saying how one is obligated by force of habit or by awe.

At another place,

The sovereign, which by both divine and natural law, alone has the function of preserving and safeguarding the laws of the state, possesses a perfect right to make any decree about religion it thinks fit, and that all are bound to obey these decrees and commands by reason of the pledge they have given it, a pledge which God bids men keep with all scrupulousness.[36]

More explanation is required here: Spinoza has defined many of the terms used in this place in a special sense. The passage may be translated: "The sovereign has the power to make laws about religion; subjects not only can be forced to comply with those laws but are rational in so complying." This is true even when the rulers are infidels. The subject,

since he has made a contract, and has transferred his right to them, then, since he has thereby surrendered the right to defend himself and his religion, he is bound [*obtemperare tenentur*] to obey them, and to honour his pledge or be compelled to honour it.[37]

It is evident that the word "bound" here means "must." The text continues:

unless God, by a sure revelation of his will, has promised him particular aid against a tyrant, or has exempted him by name.[38]

Three distinct levels of meaning are discernible in this passage:

[36] TTP, XVI, 147.
[37] *Ibid.*
[38] *Ibid.*

a. On the surface it is a reassurance to the religious reader and illustrates the extreme delicacy necessary in religious discussion in Spinoza's time. Protestant readers scorned Catholic miracle-mongering and the claim of the Popes to control national monarchs. It was not too dangerous, then, for Hobbes, Spinoza, and later, Hume, to disavow a belief in miracles and to teach the doctrine of the supremacy of the secular state. The problem arose when these same Protestants recalled that their own faith was based on ancient miracles and on the right of the Apostles to defy the Roman authorities. It cost Hobbes and Spinoza little to make a special case of this scruple; [39] the intelligent reader would see at once that so arbitrary an exception was an empty conciliatory gesture.

b. The "unless" in the last passage is a condition contrary to fact, as readers of the *Ethics* will know. Spinoza's God makes no promises or particular revelations of his will; he exempts no one by name. The exception is an empty category.[40]

c. The passage makes good Spinozistic sense, however, if we translate it to read: "unless someone has the actual power to struggle effectively against a tyrant."

The word "oblige" in Spinoza's writings will always be found to mean either "must" or "is well advised to." Spinoza's theological terminology must always, in accordance with his own instructions, be translated into naturalistic language.

Among commentators and historians, there is general agreement that Spinoza has discarded moral obligation. There are, however, no lack of objections to his having done so and some misapprehensions of his meaning.

Martineau not only believes that there is "a total failure of all ethical conditions" in Spinoza's system, but that even prudential obligation is there impossible, because "there is . . . no provision in Spinoza's universe for personal causation or com-

[39] TTP, XVI, 145; TTP, XIX, 215.
[40] TTP (Dover), I, 13, 28; TTP (Dover), Pref., p. 4.

mand of an alternative, or action for an end as distinguished from action from a force." [41] Even John Dewey's reduced "end-in-view" version of Spinoza's exemplar concept disposes of this objection. An end-in-view is part of the package of efficient causes which impels us onward.

Bidney notes that:

Spinoza counsels the Socratic virtue of absolute obedience to the laws of the state even though such idealism involves certain death. A free man must never act in bad faith.[42]

and believes that

Spinoza's Stoic rationalism with its acknowledgement of absolute moral standards is incompatible with his biological naturalism which teaches the complete relativity of all good and evil, virtue and vice, to the requirements of self-preservation.[43]

Neither Socrates nor Spinoza really advocates absolute obedience to the laws of the state, and the implication that Spinoza holds absolute moral values or standards in any ordinary sense comparable to those of Stoic rationalism—and were the moral standards of the latter quite so absolute? [44]—seems surprising. What is most surprising in Bidney's statement is his apparent failure to grasp what surely is one of the central points in Spinoza's ethical doctrine: that although good and evil, virtue and vice, are indeed relative to the requirements of self-preservation, that self-preservation is itself not merely biological, relative only to continued physical functioning, but refers most strongly to the preservation of the essential self. The student of Spinoza who does not grasp this point cannot but believe that philosopher to be strangely incoherent.

Vaughan says that "what we have to assume, then, is a

[41] *Types of Ethical Theory,* pp. 369–72.
[42] Pp. 316–17.
[43] *Ibid.*
[44] Jaffa, p. 62.

community from which all belief in duty, in any kind of moral obligation, is rigidly barred out," [45] and continues for twenty more pages to show that such a society will not work, because so few men attain the moral level of a Spinoza. This is a striking misrepresentation of the text on the part of so acute a critic. Spinoza nowhere implies that the concept of moral obligation should be ruled out of society. On the contrary, he says explicitly that the mass of people can only be ruled by such means as religion, awe, habit, and obedience.[46] It is true that he believes it would be better if they could be governed through their own enlightened self-interest; his political goal is the improvement of men so that they can be so ruled and so rule themselves. But it was Spinoza himself who objected to those who "conceive men, not as they are, but as they would like them to be." [47] Worse, Vaughan almost ignores Spinoza's view that moral obligation is not theoretically defensible, and argues as though the social need for a sense of moral duty made it also philosophically tenable.[48]

There is a criticism which seems not to have been made but which expresses a combination of Bidney's thought, above, and a few lines on moral obligation in Plamenatz.[49] This argument, while it admits that Spinoza is correct in showing that there can be nothing either external to us, such as a command or a power, or internal, such as a promise, which can be morally binding, yet maintains that if prudential or physical obligation is to replace moral obligation it must not do so by way of reduction, but must include everything that is meant by moral obligation. But, as Plamenatz points out, the essence of moral obligation is that it implies that *we condemn ourselves* for a breach of it.

[45] *Studies*, I, 93.
[46] Wolf, *Correspondence*, Ep. 43, p. 257: "Therefore he asserts falsely that I declare that there is no room left for precepts and commands . . ."
[47] TP, I, par. 1.
[48] Smith, at pp. 40–41, makes the same error.
[49] I, 128.

Consider an example: A small act of discourtesy to a stranger in a distant city is condemned both by those who believe we have a moral obligation and by those who think we have a prudential obligation not to act in this way. The remorse we may feel for it, however, even much later, is accounted for by a theory of moral obligation on the ground that a moral principle has been transgressed; it seems not to be accounted for by Spinoza's utilitarian, prudential theory. In fact, Spinoza condemns such remorse flatly,[50] although he allows that it may have a value in prompting us not to repeat the act. It may be, however, that the idea that such remorse is justified is one of the stubbornnesses of human character to which philosophers must bow; if Spinoza does not account for it without denying it, he is mistaken. However, Spinoza does account for it, not directly through the principle of utility, but through the exemplar concept. The disproportion between my regret for a small unkindness and its objective external effects as judged by utility theory is accounted for by the fact that my failure to live up to my idea of what I might be, my exemplar, cannot readily be explained except on the hypothesis that I am indeed far from my ideal; this is a serious blow to the euphoric ego-enhancement accompanying my ordinary view of myself as one approaching autonomy.

What, then, is the important practical difference between Spinoza's attempt to reach an ideal and the attempt of another to meet a moral obligation, between Spinoza's recommendations for self-preservation and, say, the Stoic ideal? In the sphere of action it may not be very great. Spinoza is no transvaluer of morals, no ethical innovator such as Nietzsche was, or such as was the Christ who said, "Ye have heard that it was said by them of old time . . . but I say unto you. . . ."[51] Only wryly can we equate Spinoza with that other Christ who said "Think not that I am come to destroy the law, or the

---

[50] E, IV, prop. 54.
[51] Matt. 5:21–22.

prophets: I am not come to destroy, but to fulfil," [52] for although Spinoza wrote as though under the tutelage of one tradition, he concluded in the sense of another. His attempt was to rewrite the "perennial philosophy" in naturalistic terms. Whether naturalistic ethics are possible is a question beyond the scope of this study, though I venture the opinion that they are, and further, that Spinoza's version of them is the most logically coherent, faithfully naturalistic, and profoundly ethical of all such systems that have been offered since his time.

[52] Matt. 5:17; TTP, V, 91.

XI

Applications

❖

International Relations

IN his doctrine of international relations, Spinoza is a straight-forward Hobbist:

Two states are in the same relation to one another as two men in the condition of nature; with this exception, that a commonwealth can guard itself against being subjugated by another, as a man in the state of nature cannot do. For, of course, a man is overcome by sleep every day, is often afflicted by disease of body or mind, and is finally prostrated by old age; in addition, he is subject to other troubles against which a commonwealth can make itself secure.[1]

Even when nations are not at war, their relative proximity and strength can bring about a practical subjection of one to another. One nation is subject to the power of another insofar as it fears it or needs its help,[2] and, as is the case with individuals in the state of nature, two states leagued together are stronger than each separately.

Spinoza is always on the side of peace, no less in international relations than within each state. The states of his model constitutions are all oriented toward maintaining peace with their neighbors:

No state is more stable to the impartial eye than one which is just powerful enough to preserve its own possessions, without being

[1] TP, III, par. 11.
[2] TP, III, par. 12.

able to covet those of others, and which therefore does its utmost to avoid war and maintain peace.[3]

Anticipating Rousseau's similar proposals, Spinoza has a word of hope for the internationalists:

The greater the number of commonwealths that make a treaty of peace together, the less is each to be feared by the rest, or, if you like, the less power each has of making war on the rest; each is more strictly bound to observe the conditions of peace.[4]

The dispersed aristocratic state is, of course, such a confederation. Spinoza's principle of equilibrium, so often brought into play in his constitutions, applies equally to international affairs.

Whether their powers are in equilibrium or not, nations are yet enemies by nature [5] and may at any time make war upon each other, break treaties, and ignore each other's interests as they please. The general rule is that, although good faith is to be preserved as much as possible, the duty of the sovereign to preserve his own state comes before his duty to keep his word.[6] "The people's welfare is the highest law, to which all other laws, both human and divine, must be adjusted." [7]

Religion

It is sufficiently well recognized that the religious struggles of the seventeenth century often involved secular conflicts that were carried on in the language of religious controversy.

---

[3] TP, VII, par. 28.

[4] TP, III, par. 16.

[5] TP, III, par. 13.

[6] TP, III, par. 14, where Spinoza's Machiavellian *raison d'état* thesis is most clearly expounded; TTP, XVI, 139–41; TP, III, par. 17; Machiavelli, *The Prince*, Ch. XVIII, pp. 64–66; de la Court, p. 227; Meinecke, pp. 80, 90–91, 99, 140, 207, 216–23. The word "duty" in the above sentence must of course be taken in its special Spinozistic sense.

[7] TTP, XIX, 213; see also Augustine *The City of God* xxii. 6; and the discussion of Augustine's view by Deane, pp. 166–67.

Perhaps it is too well recognized, for just as present-day political analysis seems sometimes to fall into a kind of reductionist
fallacy in slurring over the power in practical affairs of ideological commitment, so historians of the seventeenth century
sometimes seem to forget that the acts of men then were often
quite simply the carrying into effect of their religious beliefs.
We know that Spinoza intended his philosophy to have a
practical effect on men's actions and also that for him the
claims of the traditional religions were, philosophically, beneath discussion; the great volume of discussion of traditional
religious matters in his formal works and correspondence can
only be accounted for by his desire to speak to men in terms
that they understood and with concepts on the basis of which
they took action.

Spinoza was one of the few in his day who saw the solution
to the conflict of church and state which was eventually
adopted: the upholding of the right of the secular power to
command outward behavior, combined with the principle of
the right of the individual to believe what he chooses, provided that his actions do not run counter to the vital interests
of the state.[8]

The solution is, of course, impossible as long as men believe
that the claims of the state and of religion are in conflict—
what rational man would imperil his salvation for the sake of
earthly advantage? Hobbes tried to show, by an ingenious but
unconvincing reinterpretation of Scripture, that the claims of
religion *do not* conflict with those of the state. Spinoza's
critique of religion cut deeper; it showed that its claims *cannot*
so conflict. The state has no concern with truth or with
opinion about truth, but cares only for men's actions. Religion
also cares nothing about truth; its sole function is the inculca-
tion of socially useful opinion: "The value of each man's faith
is to be judged only by the obedience or obstinacy which it

[8] TP, III, par. 10; TTP, VII, 109.

inspires, and not by its truth or falsity." [9] Only rational men—philosophers and scientists—are concerned with truth.

Religion was the most dangerous subject that Spinoza could discuss; [10] it is here that we must make maximum allowance for tactfulness on his part. Believing, as he did, that the Bible was but a confused collection of folktales, with no higher authority to guide our actions than, say, the Koran [11] or *Orlando Furioso*, holding a concept of God which for most men at any time would be indistinguishable from atheism, [12] and compelled to handle the religious question in all his writings, he was forced to say things in a way that would be compatible both with the truth as he saw it and with survival in a world of more than usually savage Christians. [13] That he managed this task without suffering persecution and without raising any serious problems for our understanding of his thought may be partly attributable to his early death but also constitutes no small tribute both to his courage and to his literary powers. [14]

Yet, although religion is, from the standpoint of the rational man, false, [15] it should not be discarded. [16] It plays a major political role in forming the national character at the original

[9] TTP, XIV, 117; see also TTP (Dover), Pref., p. 9; TTP, III, 59; TTP (Dover), XIII, 180; TTP, XIV, 123: "the sole aim of philosophy is truth: the sole aim of faith obedience and piety."

[10] Wolf, *Correspondence*, Ep. 42, p. 239.

[11] *Ibid.*, p. 254; TTP (Dover), X, 150.

[12] Colerus, p. 66: "the God of Spinoza is a meer Phantom, an imaginary God, who is nothing less than God."

[13] TTP (Dover), Pref., pp. 6–7.

[14] The student of Spinoza should be able to translate into naturalistic terms the passage at TTP (Dover), XII, 172–73: "that a God exists, that He foresees all things, that He is Almighty, that by His decree the good prosper and the wicked come to naught, and, finally, that our salvation depends solely on His Grace"; see also the equivocal use of the term "superstition," at TTP (Dover), Pref., pp. 3–4.

[15] "False," insofar as it pretends to rational truth. This is the meaning of the part of the *Tractatus Theologico-Politicus* where Spinoza tries to demonstrate the independence of philosophy from theology. Some religious ideas do, of course, contain or imply philosophical truths—accidentally. See TTP, IV, 87, and TTP (Dover), XIII, 176.

[16] TTP, V, 89; TTP (Dover), XV, 197–98.

founding of the state. The need for religion diminishes, but is not wholly lost, as the state gains support from other sources—rational self-interest, patriotic fervor, and the inertia of habitual compliance, for instance. The social, and only, function of religion at all times is to teach obedience to the rational demands of society by those persons who cannot be compelled or rationally persuaded.[17]

In the formative period of the state, the goodness of a religion consists in the effectiveness with which it serves its purpose of producing national unity. In the later and more developed state, although religion still serves a necessary end, it may be important that the particular form of the religion not offer a serious barrier to the further advancement of subjects toward rationality.[18] In the ideal state implicit in Spinoza's thought, religion might cease to exist at all.[19]

If religion is to perform its political mission well, it must be under the control of the political authority: "the holders of sovereign power are the depositaries and interpreters of religious no less than of civil ordinances."[20] Under no circumstances ought a religion or a religious doctrine requiring ecclesiastical interpretation be allowed an independent authority within the state.[21]

---

[17] Machiavelli, *Discourses*, I, Chs. 11–12, pp. 240–44; Rousseau, *Social Contract*, Bk. II, Ch. 7, pp. 40–41. It would be proper for the modern reader to translate "religion" as "ideology" or "cult of nationalism." Spinoza is here typically an Enlightenment man in seeing the religious myth as socially integrative and in not seeing it as psychically integrative.

[18] It was a commonplace of seventeenth-century thought that Protestantism and commerce had affinities and there was much speculation about the predisposing influences of different religions on secular characteristics.

[19] TTP, V, 95; TTP (Dover), Pref., p. 5: "But if, in despotic statecraft, the supreme and essential mystery be to hoodwink the subjects, and to mask the fear, which keeps them down, with the specious garb of religion . . . in a free state no more mischievous expedient could be planned or attempted."

[20] TTP (Dover), Pref., p. 10; see also TTP, XVI, 147; TTP, XIX, 205, 211, 217; TP, III, par. 10.

[21] TTP, XIV, 111; TTP, XVIII, 191, 197: "How disastrous it is for both religion and the state to give ministers of religion any right to make decrees or to handle state affairs . . ."; TTP, XIX, 205.

The sovereign must preempt the authority to interpret religious doctrine lest someone else use it against him.[22] But this right only goes so far as the right to regulate outward actions. Spinoza exempts inward religion from state control [23] and even the interpretation of Scripture insofar as it relates to belief only.[24] He means the religious ordinances of the sovereign to be very general and permissive; religious dogmatism and persecution are disastrous to the state.[25]

Some retreat even from this position may be evidenced where Spinoza sets forth the state-church relation in his model monarchy:

As regards religion, no churches whatsoever are to be built at the cities' expense; nor should laws be passed against religious beliefs unless they are seditious and radically subversive. Thus those who are permitted to practise their religion openly may, if they wish, build a church at their own expense. That the king may practise the religion which he favors he should have a chapel of his own in the palace.[26]

The retreat, if there is one, is slight. In speaking of religion in the aristocratic state, Spinoza reaffirms what he said earlier:

My views on religion have been fully expounded in the *Tractatus Theologico-Politicus*, and it only remains to add one or two points which were beyond the scope of that work. The first is that all patricians should be of the same faith, the very simple universal faith set out in the treatise referred to.[27]

[22] TTP, XIX, 217; TTP, XIX, 221–23: The sovereign must control the interpretation of the national ideology. In Spinoza's time, the national monarchs had to control, evade, or repel the authority of the Pope to interpret the national religion, as today the Chinese feel the necessity of denying the authority of Moscow to interpret the Marxist text.
[23] TTP, VII, 109.
[24] TTP (Dover), VII, 119.
[25] TTP, XIV, 111.
[26] TP, IV, par. 40.
[27] TP, VIII, par. 46. The reference is to TTP, XIV, 119, and to TTP (Dover), Pref., p. 10.

The "simple universal faith" referred to is described [28] as a belief in a single, omniscient, all-powerful God, who forgives the sins of the penitent, and whose worship "consists solely in justice and charity (or love) towards one's neighbor." [29] Only those who obey God in this manner are saved. It is evident that even this simple religion is not Spinoza's own.[30]

The unity of religion necessary in an aristocracy is required of the patricians only; its simplicity is a guard against the growth of divisive dogmatic sects and against the possibility of a superstitious or bigoted aristocratic class persecuting the plebeians and so weakening the state.[31] The subjected classes are to have complete freedom to voice their beliefs, although the churches of dissenters are to be small and scattered, while the churches of the state religion should be large and magnificient and manned by the patriciate.[32]

As for religion in a democracy, "in a society where sovereignty is vested in all, and laws are made by common consent, obedience has no place." [33] If the sole function of religion is to teach obedience, then it would appear that religion is not needed in a democracy. This would probably represent an ideal case; for an actual democracy, such as he began to describe at the end of the *Tractatus Politicus*, it seems very likely that Spinoza would have recommended a single, universally obligatory, and very general creed—as did Rousseau.[34]

Spinoza attempted to prove his religious conclusions from Scripture itself. The attempt founded the art or science of

[28] TTP, XIV, 119: "all dogmas that can give rise to controversy among good men are excluded."

[29] TTP (Dover), Pref., p. 9; see also TTP (Dover), VII, 104; TTP (Dover), XII, 172.

[30] TTP, XIV, 121.

[31] TTP, XIV, 111.

[32] There is some relationship between Spinoza's religious arrangements in his model aristocracy and the actual state of affairs in the Netherlands before 1672. Most of the regents leaned toward a liberal Protestantism which might be described as "a simple universal faith."

[33] TTP, V, 95.

[34] *Social Contract*, Bk. IV, Ch. 8, p. 139.

biblical criticism [35] and is both interesting and important in its own right; it is not, however, sufficiently relevant to the present political study to warrant discussion here.

We know from his biography and writings that Spinoza rejected Judaism, and in a letter he denounces Catholicism as a vulgar superstition.[36] He lived with a sect of Mennonites for a while shortly after his excommunication from the synagogue; the suggestion has been made that his thought bears traces of Anabaptism and German mysticism. However true this may be of Spinoza's ethics, it seems certain that the distinctly anti-political stand of most Anabaptists was not compatible with his own views.

Spinoza's relationship to Calvinism is a more intricate matter. Here we must distinguish between the Calvinist churches in the Netherlands and Calvinism as a system of thoughts and attitudes.

Obviously, the Dutch Calvinists and Spinoza were natural enemies. It was this sect which had both the will and the power to threaten him, his writings, and his friends; he lived in the shadow of that threat all of his life. He saw the orthodox Calvinists as a major force for political and intellectual regression in the Netherlands; he attacked them frontally and by indirection throughout all his writings. Sometimes the attacks are so indirect that we need some knowledge of contemporary circumstances in order to understand the text. For example, he remarks in the *Ethics* [37] that "providing for the poor is a duty which falls on the State as a whole," and elsewhere [38] he says that no one has the right to provide for the poor except by the authority or permission of the sovereign. These statements, apparently gratuitous in context, become meaningful when

[35] Hubbeling, p. 61: "Spinoza formulated for the first time in history the principles of historical critical hermeneutics."
[36] Wolf, *Correspondence*, Ep. 76, pp. 350–55.
[37] E, IV, App. 17.
[38] TTP, XIX, 217.

we learn that the Calvinist clergy had a large hand in the distribution of poor-relief funds and that they used this position for political advantage.[39]

On the other hand, Calvinism was also a climate of opinion which emphasized personal religious experience over ritual and the authority of conscience over that of tradition. Its doctrines included a denial of free will, the assertion that salvation, when had, is obtained without personal merit, the reaffirmation of the unity and power of God and of the dependence of all things on him, and even, as Calvin himself put it, the idea that the state is to "bring it to pass that God may rule over us." Ideas of this sort were not confined to nominally Calvinist sects, they infiltrated other Protestant churches, they crept into French Catholicism by way of Jansenism, and even into the Amsterdam synagogues.

It is, therefore, not farfetched to consider Spinozism as, in some respects, a secularized Calvinism. The self-evident authenticity of the personal religious experience is comparable to the self-certifying character of Spinoza's clear and simple ideas and the kind of knowledge had by direct intuition. Of the many other affinities, I should like to suggest two, both highly speculative. The first is psychological and has to do with the combination of millenarianism and advocacy of an intense social and moral discipline in the two systems. The other has to do with the functional relationship of Calvinist "conscience" and Spinozistic "reason." Each is the ultimate resource of individual men; each supplies both the justification for disobedience and the command to conformity; both are common and at least potentially uniform in all men and point to the possibility of an actual community of saints. It was left to Rousseau, the disciple of both Calvin and Spinoza, to synthesize and politicize the two terms.[40]

[39] Boxer, p. 9; Zumthor, pp. 250–51.
[40] *Social Contract*, Bk. II, Ch. 7, p. 39.

Civil Liberty and Political Freedom

It has been said above that the end of man, according to his essence, is understanding, that to the extent to which he reaches understanding he also finds freedom, and that the state, as an agency of man's desires, is similarly directed toward freedom. We have learned to be wary of some uses of the word "freedom," however; it is desirable to see what Spinoza meant by it in his political thought.

Retrospectively, it can be seen that the problem of the seventeenth-century bourgeoisie was to support a centralized national state which would provide stability and the protection from local harassment necessary for commerce, without at the same time raising up a Leviathan which would devour them.[41]

As against the national state, the older conception of freedom would not serve without also supporting the feudal order in which it had originated. Liberty and right had then been seen to arise only out of contract or status in the social order. The more recently arrived at theory of the freedom of the individual conscience to interpret the word of God was not only of too narrow a scope to be applicable to the whole spectrum of political encroachments from above, it also threatened both orders, the old and the new.

A device which had some roots in both religious and feudal concepts of freedom was the ideology of the rights of man. The Leviathan would be tamed if the principle could be demonstrated, and enforced, that each man has specific innate rights to such things as life, liberty, and property.

The principle can be enforced, it appears, only when it is tied to a more powerful social principle, such as that of *laissez faire*, with which the fortunes of the rights-of-man theory have been intimately connected; it can be demonstrated only by recourse to natural law or theology.

[41] No seventeenth-century writer that I know understood matters in quite these terms; the observation is offered as a useful oversimplification.

As we have seen, Spinoza's definition of natural right excludes the rights-of-man thesis. He fell back, then, for protection against the arbitrary state, on constitutionalism and on a theory of the self-limiting character of political power. If it is proper to argue from the current consensus, we may point out that Spinoza's advocacy of constitutionalism is still sound doctrine, whereas in rejecting the support of the rhetoric of natural rights he abandoned a reed which, despite its great propaganda value in the past, has since proven frail as a principle.[42]

Spinoza's statement that man abandons his freedom or natural right when he leaves the state of nature must be taken with caution. The freedom or right lost is but an empty right to do anything under circumstances where almost nothing can in fact be done.

Human right or freedom is a nonentity as long as it is an individual possession determined by individual power; it exists in imagination rather than in fact, since there is no certainty of making it good. Nor can it be disputed that the more cause for fear an individual has, the less power he has, and in consequence the less right he has. Besides, it is hardly possible for men to maintain life and cultivate the mind without mutual help. I therefore conclude that the right of nature peculiar to human beings can scarcely be conceived save where men hold rights as a body.[43]

The question of freedom perhaps ought not enter here; what is really significant is the question of power. In leaving the state of nature the individual has removed himself from an isolation in which he "could do anything" and entered a

---

[42] Natural right theory, in the form in which it was held from the late seventeenth to the early nineteenth centuries, was a very powerful principle in actual politics. Its survival of the successive refutations of Hobbes, Spinoza, Hume, Burke, Bentham, and Hegel is an impressive tribute to the capacity of political man to believe what is convenient to him. Yet, despite its present low estate, it would be rash to predict that it will not again come into use or that it cannot be intelligently reformulated.

[43] TP, II, par. 15; see also E, IV, prop. 73.

society in which, though he can still do "anything," the conditions under which he exercises that right have changed. The man in the state of nature has powers restricted only, but very greatly, by the physical circumstances of his situation. The powers of the man in civil society are diminished in some ways by the commands, or demands, of the state, but they are greatly enlarged in other ways. The end result is a greater net power for the individual;[44] each man has command of the whole power of society for certain purposes of his own, at the price of adding his power to the common store for the benefit of others. An increase in the power, the absoluteness, of the state is therefore paralleled by an increase in the power of the subject, and so also by an increase in his right or freedom, even though some of his particular powers—to evade or defy the law—diminish.[45] The state is not the natural enemy of the freedom of men but their rational tool.

This construction is completely abstract and not open to objections based on observation—such as that man is born free and yet is everywhere in chains.[46] Spinoza is aware of the miseries that the state can inflict on its subjects, but he never loses sight of his idea that it is yet the principal agency of man's salvation.[47]

Spinoza does not treat at length of the matter of the civil rights or liberties of citizens in any one place, nor can his idea of those rights be set forth briefly. We might first consider a contradiction into which he has seemed to fall. It will be recalled that in Epistle 50 Spinoza stated that "I always preserve natural right intact" both in the state of nature and in civil society. How, then, can he say:

[44] TP, II, par. 13.

[45] TP, III, par. 2.

[46] Rousseau, who thought that the state had put men in chains, advocated a better state, not the abolition of states. Anarchists, who believe that all states put men in chains, though they have redefined the meaning of "society" and put society in opposition to the state, yet give indirectly to society all the powers that Spinoza requires for his abstract idea of the state.

[47] TTP, XIX, 213; TP, V, par. 4; E, IV, prop. 40.

Whoever has transferred his power to defend himself to another, whether voluntarily or under constraint, has undoubtedly divested himself of his natural right completely, and in consequence has determined to obey the other in everything without exception . . .[48]

The citizen has not retained his own right but is subject to the right of the commonwealth, and is bound to carry out every one of its commands; clear also that he has no right to decide what is fair or unfair, moral or immoral . . . no matter how unfair a subject considers the decrees of the commonwealth to be, he is bound to carry them out.[49]

Verbally, of course, the contradiction is not apparent but real. This is the only occasion on which we must reject Spinoza's *ipsissima verba* in order to preserve his thought. The thought is that men are free to do at all times whatever they choose and are able to do, and that both in the state of nature and in civil society the conditions of life, and in the civil society the conditions of law, limit their choices very drastically. It is in emphasizing one or the other aspect of this thought that Spinoza appears to fall into a confusion.

The state has, of course, the power and therefore the right to impose its will upon the subject in every possible way, but

a commonwealth is most powerful, and most fully possessed of its own right, if it is based on and guided by reason. Now since the best way to preserve oneself as far as possible is to live as reason prescribes, a man or a commonwealth always acts in the best way when it is most fully possessed of its own right. I do not assert that everything which I say is done by right is done in the best way. It is one thing to cultivate a field by right, and another to cultivate it in the best way; it is one thing, I say, to defend and preserve oneself, to give judgement and so on by right, another to defend and preserve oneself in the best way, and to give the best

[48] TTP, XVI, 137.
[49] TP, III, par. 5.

judgement. In consequence, it is one thing to rule and have charge of public affairs by right, another to rule and direct public affairs in the best way.[50]

That is, because the ruler is bound, as all are, to serve his own interests, he is also bound to serve them really, that is, in as intelligent a way as is possible for him. Because the power of the ruler is the effective sum of the power of his subjects, it is to his interest to favor those measures which make the subjects most free, rational, inventive, and enterprising, as well as most attached to the state and to each other.[51] Thus the state weakens itself if its laws are unjust or senseless,[52] or if it persecutes dissenters.

Rebellions, wars, and contemptuous disregard for law must certainly be attributed to the corrupt condition of the commonwealth rather than to the wickedness of its subjects. For citizens are not born but made. Besides, men's natural passions are the same everywhere; hence if wickedness is more dominant and crime more prevalent in one commonwealth than in another, this is certainly due to the fact that the first has not done enough to promote harmony, has not framed its laws with sufficient foresight, and so has failed to acquire its absolute right as a commonwealth.[53]

More strongly,

The more the sovereign tries to deprive men of freedom of speech, the more stubbornly is it opposed; not indeed by money-grubbers, sycophants, and the rest of the shallow crew, whose supreme happiness is to gloat over the coins in their coffers and to have their bellies well-stuffed, but by those who, because of their culture, integrity, and ability, have some independence of mind.[54]

[50] TP, V, par. 1.
[51] TP, VII, par. 5.
[52] TP, II, par. 21.
[53] TP, V, par. 1; see also TTP, XVII, 173.
[54] TTP, XX, 235-37; see also TTP (Dover), Pref., pp. 5-6.

Finally, the state is in real need of the advice of its citizens in governing them; this advice cannot be had if citizens are not permitted to speak freely.[55]

There are three superficial explanations of Spinoza's divergence from his libertarianism. First, Spinoza has overcommitted himself to Hobbes and sometimes is led to make stronger statements about the power of the state than, given the peculiarities of his own outlook, he should. Second, revolution in the Netherlands meant the victory of reaction. The libertarian revolution had taken place in the sixteenth century; Spinoza had a vested interest against further revolution in his own country.[56] Third, Spinoza's theory of the national character led him to believe that revolutions did not commonly succeed in their purposes; a monarchical people could not rid themselves of monarchy but only of particular monarchs; people usually had the kind of government that suited their character.

None of these explanations seems adequate. In an article not otherwise distinguished by perceptivity, T. V. Smith suggests that Spinoza "was feeling his way to a distinction between government and sovereignty." [57] The thought is provocative: we may understand that in counseling unlimited support for the state, Spinoza really has the principle of sovereignty in mind; in pointing to the right of revolution, he is thinking of the dispensability of particular rulers, regimes, or constitutions. Subjects may revolt against the sovereign in the name of the sovereignty. As a matter of practice, this was not new. The English Parliament, some twenty-five years ago, had levied war on Charles I in the name of the King, and earlier

[55] TP, VII, par. 5; Coser, p. 153: "Groups which are not involved in continued struggle with the outside are less prone to make claims on total personality involvement of the membership and are more likely to exhibit flexibility of structure. The multiple internal conflicts which they tolerate may in turn have an equilibrating and stabilizing impact on the structure."
[56] Geyl, Part 1, p. 70.
[57] P. 39.

precedents are numerous. The principle was not fully worked out until Rousseau.

Gough believes that Spinoza sees the people as transferring power, natural right, to society rather than to a ruler.[58] Duff understands that "men do transfer their power to the community as a whole, and not to one or a few men." [59] Spinoza remarks that

at meetings of public authorities, both sovereign and subordinate, it is rare for anything to be done by the unanimous vote of all the members, yet everything *is* done by the common decision of all, of those that is, who voted against the measure as well as of those who voted for it.[60]

The Latin original seems stronger: "*et tamen omnia ex communi omnium decreto . . .*"

No one can give up his natural right to do what is best for himself. It is always best for each man that he not be in the state of nature, that there be a sovereign. It is never reasonable, therefore, to oppose the existence of sovereignty. It might at times, however, be reasonable to oppose the actual holder of sovereign power, on the ground that he hinders or defeats the aim of sovereignty itself. There are hints of this thought in writers before Spinoza, but Rousseau seems to have expressed it most completely in his doctrine of the general will. Perhaps this later development can be more completely understood if we see it in terms of an explication of what is implicit in Spinoza's political thought.[61]

What about the case of the individual living in a state whose

[58] P. 108.

[59] P. 284; see also pp. 283 and 366: "We have already seen that the power of a State . . . is unity of mind, or common will."

[60] TTP, XX, 233.

[61] Kline, p. 10: "Maxim Kovalevski, . . . focused attention on Spinoza as a political thinker whose doctrines were 'an essential link in the development of the theory of popular sovereignty,' anticipating Rousseau and the later social-contract theorists on many important points"; TP, II, par. 16; TP, II, par. 21.

ruler is much less enlightened than he himself is? [62] If we assume that he is an isolated person, or a member of a small group, it is evident that his rights or powers against the state are negligible. What, under these circumstances, are we to make of the case of a Thoreau? Even if we suppose that he had a rational apprehension of the undesirability of slavery and of the support of that institution by the national government, how, in terms of Spinoza's principles, are we to understand Thoreau's action in going to jail rather than pay taxes to that government? Admittedly he had a right, a power, not to prevent the government from supporting slavery, but to refuse to support the government. Further, it may be said that he was obliged to act as he did in the light of his understanding—even Thoreau did not have free will. The question is, was his understanding correct? We may give him the benefit of the doubt in his belief that the law was irrational. Was his own action rational?

That it was not rational might seem evident on the basis of a partial reading of Spinoza, who asserted that rebellion is irrational because the state is the necessary condition of survival and progress, who saw the seventeenth-century equivalent of Thoreau in the inspired religious fanatic armed with the inner light and dangerous to all government, good or bad, who said that even irrational laws and tyrants should be obeyed.[63] To the extent that Spinoza is a Hobbist he must say that Thoreau was mistaken in his action.

Spinoza is more than a Hobbist, however, and insofar as in places he says that action against government is always mistaken he goes beyond the spirit of his own thought. Thoreau

---

[62] Duff, p. 3, sees a contrast between Aristotle, who believed that individual virtue was a product of the state, and Spinoza, who saw the good state as a product of individual virtue. It would seem more accurate to understand Spinoza to be saying that good citizens, or good men, and good states are reciprocally causes and effects of each other; see also, Aristotle on the tension between the concepts "good citizen" and "good man"; *Politics* 1288a.

[63] TTP, XIX, 213.

resisted the tax but not the imprisonment. His action was meant as a kind of speech rather than as a kind of defiance; [64] he falls into the category of those who give testimony.[65] Giving testimony can vary from Pilate's washing of his hands to the self-immolation of a Buddhist monk in a village square, that is, from a gesture of disengagement to an attempt, necessarily personally expensive, to arouse the conscience of a government or of a people. The case of Socrates is, of course, identical, for although much has been made of his obedience in refusing to escape the punishment of his native city, it should also be recalled that he firmly refused to comply with her demand that he stop testifying to the truth that he saw.[66]

The point at which bearing witness verges into subversion of government itself, or produces a net undesirable effect is not precisely determinable. Even the best man is not completely rational nor does he know the total effect of his actions. Even bad causes have their martyrs, and good causes have adherents whose actions, in their effect, are indistinguishable from those of *agents provocateurs*. The rationality of an act is determined not only by the rationality of its intent but also by the probability of its attaining the end in view. Practical judgment and imaginative insight may both fail to direct us; the consensus of reasonable men, over a period of time, if that is what is meant by the "judgment of history," may be the only criterion of action, but it comes too late—if at all. There is no rule in Spinoza's system for determining when and how much to resist government; the external struggle between tory and revolutionary is also carried on within the mind of the thoughtful man who wishes both to preserve what has been achieved and to improve it.[67]

[64] TTP, XX, 231.

[65] TTP, XVII, 173–75.

[66] Hume, *Political Essays*, pp. 60–61: "Socrates refuses to escape from prison because he had tacitly promised to obey the laws. Thus he builds a *Tory* consequence of passive obedience on a *Whig* foundation of the original contract."

[67] Locke, *Two Treatises of Government*, p. 323: "I my self can only be Judge in my own Conscience."

The passages where Spinoza speaks of the "right" of revolution are numerous: [68]

Men have never surrendered their right and transferred their
power so completely that they ceased to be feared by the very
rulers who received their right and power, and, although de-
prived of their natural right, became less dangerous to the state
as citizens than its external enemies.[69]

Men endowed with reason never renounce their right so completely that they cease to be men and can be treated like sheep.[70]

Since no one can so utterly abdicate his own power of self-
defence as to cease to be a man, I conclude that subjects, either by
tacit agreement, or by social contract, retain a certain number [of
rights] which cannot be taken from them without great danger to
the state.[71]

This last passage, it will be noticed, raises in the phrase
"tacit agreement" a semblance of the theory of innate rights,
only to quash it with the concluding phrase which bases all on
the danger to the state.

Spinoza's actions themselves, which always displayed re-
markable conformity with his principles, give perhaps the best
testimony of what his system implies. The last paragraph of
the *Tractatus Theologico-Politicus* begins:

My treatise being now complete, it only remains to say expressly
that it contains nothing which I would not willingly submit to the
examination and judgement of my country's rulers. If anything I
have written is in their judgement contrary to my country's laws
or detrimental to the general welfare, I am ready to retract it.[72]

---

[68] TP, IV, par. 5; Rousseau, *Social Contract*, Bk. I, Ch. 4, p. 8; there is no
moral "right" of revolution for Spinoza, of course. For a rational man, revolution is justified by sufficient reason and good chance of success—success,
meaning not only victory but a better government following the one against
which he revolts.
[69] TTP, XVII, 149; see also TTP, V, 93.
[70] TP, VII, par. 25.
[71] TTP (Dover), Pref., p. 10.
[72] TTP, XX, 243; see also, TTP (Dover), Pref., p. 11.

The work was, of course, never submitted to "their judgement"; Spinoza knew quite well that it would fail to pass the
examination of his country's rulers. His treatise was published
without his name upon it. When the publication of a translation was proposed, Spinoza opposed it on the ground that it
would lead to condemnation of the Latin edition. The Latin
edition was condemned anyway. Spinoza's whole life is a
qualification, if not an outright rejection, of the notion that
the subject "has no right to decide what is fair or unfair, moral
or immoral." [73]

[73] TP, III, par. 5; TTP (Dover), XIV, 189; Santayana, *Introduction*, p.
xvi; Martineau, *A Study of Spinoza*, p. 38, retells the story that Spinoza
once made a self-portrait which shows him in the costume of Masaniello,
the leader of the insurgent Neapolitan populace. All anecdotes of Spinoza
point to him as more of a political activist than his writings might indicate.

XII

Conclusion

❖

AMONG the principal achievements of Spinoza, at the levels of
metaphysics, ethics, and political philosophy are: the conversion of a great metaphysical tradition into a philosophy of science, the creation of a naturalistic ethics, and the reconciliation
of the claims of individual freedom and social peace through
an analysis of the nature of political power. The premise of
the foregoing exposition of these and other matters is that
their interconnections and full meaning are best set forth by
proceeding deductively, from the general to the particular. A
topical treatment is also possible, however, as I propose now to
illustrate in a very summary fashion.

There is, first, the matter of Spinoza's own personality. It is
as opaque to us as that of Plato or Shakespeare. Their biogra-
phies tell us nothing, although we come away from the works
with a sense of having encountered a union of incredible
power and subtlety. We can struggle to comprehend the
subtlety; it is our own mind operating with ideal efficiency.
The power unnerves us. It arises out of a fundamental direct-
ness and simplicity of understanding and intent that bear small
likeness to the combination of rigid compulsiveness and dispersed vacillation we encounter in our own minds. Spinoza is,
as much as other men, a legitimate object of psychological
study, but the fate of previous attempts to plumb his mind does
not promote a desire to expose the shallowness of my own in
the attempt.

Other approaches may prove more useful. We can begin by considering Spinoza as an apologist for the DeWitt regime and for the class of regents it represented. No evidence contradicts this view and it is strongly supported by a comparative study of the *Tractatus Theologico-Politicus* and de la Court's *True Interest and Political Maxims of the Republic of Holland*, a book which is completely dedicated to the DeWitt cause. The two books appeared at about the same time, met the same political emergency, and agree on so many matters of opinion, although at different levels of generality, that a large mutuality of purpose must be assumed. Further, not only in the *Tractatus Politicus* but even in the *Ethics* we encounter numerous arguments and asides which can only be understood and accounted for as supportive of the DeWitt party. Finally, all of Spinoza's Dutch friends were members of that party and all of the biographical data indicate that his political partisanship was not only intellectual but emotional. His criticisms of regent government, which he thought of as aristocratic, are criticisms of its tactical errors, not of its principles. It is true that he favored the democratic over the aristocratic ideal, but the actual alternatives in his time were not democracy or some other form of government, but feudal particularism, Papal or Calvinist dualism, and Anabaptist anarchy, on the one hand, and on the other, the efficient, secularized, omnicompetent modern state. There were two models of the modern state. One was the small, oligarchic, commercial city-state exemplified by Holland and Venice; the other was the dynastic monarchy of France, extensive, populous, and predominantly agricultural. England was in between: London, plus some other commercial cities made up a kind of Holland within a rural economy which was a kind of France; the interaction of the two components was unpredictable. Spinoza supported the commercial urban republic model against that of the territorial monarchy. For the seventeenth, if not for the twentieth century, he was overruled. As for his ideal of democracy,

Spinoza's preference of aristocratic over monarchic government represented acceptance of a second-best constitution,
but with the idea that an effective aristocratic system is a
way-station on the road to democracy. The thought is similar
to that of J. S. Mill, who favored democracy as an ultimate
goal, but urged a broadly-based, liberal, and educating oligarchic regime as the interim objective. We know, and Spinoza
guessed, that constitutional monarchy may also lead to democracy, yet the probability of this event, as a seventeenth-
century observer might have calculated it, was not very great.

The Protestant ethic and the spirit of capitalism found an
able defender in one of the poorest of the Sephardic Jews in
Holland. We ought not, merely because he was so much
more, withhold from Spinoza the name of bourgeois ideologist. It is beyond the limits of a paragraph to set forth the
details of his adherence to middle-class doctrines, but the
broad lines of that connection are clear: he opposed the gothic
order, the feudal aristocracy, the organic and hierarchical
analogies of society, monopoly, and the appeal to authority
and tradition. He favored individualism and free trade, open
careers for talent, and the freedoms of speech, press, and
conscience. His writings are full of anticipations of Adam
Smith, Bentham, Rousseau and of the English and French
Revolutions to come. The reader should be alert to detect
these and other evidences of what is variously known as class
bias, progressivism, or alignment with the forces of history.

As a writer on religion, Spinoza is chiefly known today as
the inventor of modern techniques of Biblical analysis. His
object, however, was to show that religion has nothing to do
with truth, that it is a "noble lie" which brings to social peace
those who cannot find their way there through their understanding. This represents not only information but a
program. Religion had become disruptive of the peace, med-
dlesome in politics, and dangerous to philosophers and scientists. Spinoza desired, not the destruction of religious institu-

tions or of the general belief in religion, but the pruning back of religious pretentions, the reduction of religion to its proper task of inculcating obedience and good citizenship. It is difficult to decide whether Spinoza thought this matter through or whether we understand his object completely. His conclusions on the meaning of religion leave no basis for rational adherence to any organized religion, not even for the Deism of the Enlightenment. Yet, if a myth is to be useful, it must be believed on other grounds than its usefulness. His program assumes a degree of insulation of rational from superstitious men which might have prevailed in Plato's *Republic,* but which rarely exists in actual societies.

In the long struggle to establish the principle of the omnicompetence of science, a principle to be sharply distinguished from that of scientism, no thinker has done more effective work than has Spinoza. Science implies the uniformity of nature and the inclusion of all things in nature. A philosophy of science cannot tolerate within its domain any concession to the principle of discontinuity, any privileged sanctuary for spirit or free will. It is not a matter of the toleration of dissent but of the maintenance of that coherence which distinguishes science from opinion. To a certain extent the progress of all disciplines, and particularly the establishment of sociology and psychology, represent a confirmation of Spinoza's metaphysics and the carrying out of his program. That program calls for progress toward the ideal of a single and comprehensive science which will mirror the attribute of thought, describe the attribute of extension, and give to men the maximum of freedom and power.

Difficulties have appeared in the realization of this program. I refer not to objections which arise out of metaphysical counter-arguments, or to problems raised by the current understanding of the relationship between deductive systems and empirical fact, or to the paradoxes of modern physics and the appealing reductionism of linguistic analysis—none of these seem conclusively to militate against taking Spinoza's system seriously, and the discussion of such matters in this place would not be appropriate. Rather, I refer to three related contemporary outlooks in the light of which his program seems overly optimistic.

The first is the unexpected complexity of social, political, and psychological phenomena, a complexity so great that the belief is common that no suitable axioms, no universally acceptable principles, will ever be discovered in those fields. Island universes of structured concepts and attached data float unattached to other parts of the same science or to other sciences or, for that matter, to any basic understanding of the common relationship of all things. For Spinoza this situation would represent a kind of polytheism.

A second wave is encountered in the current view of the term "human nature." The main difficulty here is not in connection with Spinoza's psychology of the passions or of ordinary political interaction, about which he is almost completely Hobbesian, as is most of contemporary political science, but with his derivation of ethical standards and of long-range political ends from a highly specified view of human nature. Yet the sciences of man no longer speak of "human nature"; those people who do are commonly thought to be, and commonly are, old-fashioned, if not reactionary. Nevertheless, although there are real practical and theoretical problems involved in the re-introduction of a working concept of human nature into the social sciences, there is some reason to believe that the principle objection is merely a matter of prejudice. Whatever the reason, it seems abundantly clear that without a definite conception of the nature of man, Spinoza has neither an ethics nor a political philosophy. Presumably this remark applies to us also.

The third point is a radical version of a view which is rather old. Augustine put it in terms of an original sin which darkened the minds of all men and made man's reason but one

more instrument of his own corruption. Hobbes remarked
that reason is the scout of the passions, and that when reason is
against a man, he will soon be against reason. Spinoza, too, said
much on the power of the passions to overcome reason, and
the theme is common in intellectual history. Since Hegel,
however, and in the midst of the most amazing triumphs of
the human intellect and demonstrations of the uniformity and
intelligibility of nature, a pervasive scepticism has eroded our
faith in both. What are our thoughts? Are they gaseous
superstructure, a reflex of underlying material conditions of
production? Are they compensations, sublimations, and wish
fulfillments? Are they culturally functional and relative and
historically conditioned? Is a thinking man a depraved animal? Does thought create the order it contemplates? Does
thought exist? These are good questions and they seem to
imply a denial of Spinoza's central doctrine of the objective
truth of at least some knowledge. On the other hand, some of
them seem also to imply a confirmation of his central doctrine
of psychic determinism.

Difficulties and climates of opinion are not, of course, dis-
proofs, and in any case good metaphysical systems are not
usually disproven, they simply go out of fashion, sometimes to
return with a new hemline. I do not myself look forward to a
revival of Spinozism itself so much as to a possible increased
awareness of the usefulness, perhaps even necessity for, the
kind of responsible metaphysical thought to which Spinoza
provokes us. By responsible metaphysical thought I mean only
the attempt to think on all subjects in one set of coherent
terms. It is not that philosophy can solve our problems. The
gap between eternal verities and poignant immediacies has
always been unbridgeable; it has been the burden and the
pride of thoughtful men at all times to live poised between the
two kinds of knowledge and to do it gracefully. It has been
suggested that men have turned away from philosophy for
good and will stoically endure the cosmic nausea that ac-

companies such heroic scepticism. We might believe it if we did not see that wherever philosophy has been evicted, her place is at once taken by the squat and vulgar idols of the tribe.

It is proper to conclude with some comments on Spinoza's political philosophy. Duff begins such a summary very well:

> From the premises of *The Prince* he reaches a conclusion analogous to that of the *Civitas Dei;* and on the basis of Hobbes's absolutism he builds a superstructure of popular liberties better secured than that of either Locke or Rousseau.[1]

On the matter of its nature and power, Spinoza stands with those who call the state a good and will not limit it in any way. This, of course, raises the question of individual liberty. But in this matter where some merely hoped for the best, or remarked with Hobbes that life cannot be without some inconveniences, or embraced Locke's unfounded natural rights, or, with Rousseau and Marx, found security in the postulation of an ultimately beneficient general will, Spinoza plucked the rose of liberty from the thistle of his own doctrine that natural right equals natural power. Until recently, it might have been assumed that his contrast of absolute with arbitrary power, the key to his taming of the Leviathan, could be understood as middle-class ideology, the politicization of free-trade theory. Now we see interesting signs, from maturing nonbourgeois countries, that this central political thesis of Spinoza's may have relevance to all advanced industrial nations, that it may yet become obvious that the reverse side of the coin of national power is individual freedom in a free society. This may lead us to the further idea that, although all thought may be ideological, all thought may not be "mere ideology." Perhaps Samuel Johnson went too far in saying that the Devil was the first Whig; does it not entail the probability that Whiggism will always be with us? Perhaps Franz Neu-

[1] P. 11.

mann did not go too far in suggesting that the task of political theory is to find what in political thought transcends immediacy.

It is true to say that Spinoza proceeded from the alienated individualism of *The Prince* to the communitarianism of the *Civitas Dei*, but the saying requires an explanation. The City of God is, after all, a dubious utopia. Few of us will get there; our getting there is not the result of our own actions; a necessary, but not sufficient, card of entry is a death certificate. As for Machiavelli, although much of his *Prince* can be read as a devil's handbook for getting along in a society that is largely in the state of nature, he does envision an earthly society in which mutual trust and friendship will prevail, however contrived or precarious the arrangements seem.

The ultimate political thought of Spinoza is to be found not in his Machiavellism or Hobbism, or in those constitutional proposals which he considered only as steppingstones to a farther shore, but in his ethical philosophy. It is there that we learn what constitutes our salvation and how we shall achieve it. It is our happiness to arrive at this freedom and personal integrity; it is a part of that happiness to lend a helping hand to others and together with them form a social and political order in which the greatest number, with the least difficulty and danger, can also be saved. The two goals of individual freedom and of the brotherhood of man are thus merged.

References Cited

❖

Aristotle. *The Basic Works of Aristotle.* Edited by Richard McKeon. New York: Random House, 1941.

Aubrey, John. *Brief Lives,* Vol. I. Edited by Andrew Clark. Oxford: Clarendon Press, 1898.

Augustine. *The City of God.* New York: Modern Library, 1950.

Barker, J. Ellis. *Rise and Decline of the Netherlands.* London: Smith, Elder and Co., 1906.

Bayle, Pierre. *Selections from Bayle's Dictionary.* Edited by E. A. Beller and M. duP. Lee, Jr. Princeton: Princeton University Press, 1952.

Berlin, Isaiah. "Does Political Theory Still Exist?" *Philosophy, Politics and Society,* Second Series. Edited by Peter Laslett and W. G. Runciman. Oxford: Basil Blackwell, 1962.

Bidney, David. *Psychology and Ethics of Spinoza.* New York: Russell and Russell, 1962.

Boxer, C. R. *The Dutch Seaborne Empire.* New York: Knopf, 1965.

Brenner, Charles. *An Elementary Textbook of Psychoanalysis.* New York: International Universities Press, 1955.

Brierly, M. "Psychoanalysis and Integrative Living," *Trends in Psychoanalysis.* London: Hogarth Press, 1951.

Broad, C. D. *Five Types of Ethical Theory.* New York: Humanities Press, 1951.

Brown, Norman O. *Life Against Death.* New York: Vintage Books, 1959.

Cambridge (New) Modern History, Vol. V. Cambridge: Cambridge University Press, 1961.

Cassirer, Ernst. *The Philosophy of the Enlightenment.* Boston: Beacon Press, 1955.

Clark, G. N. *The Seventeenth Century.* Oxford: Oxford University Press, 1931.

Colerus, John. *The Life of Benedict de Spinoza.* London: Benj. Bragg, 1706.

Colie, Rosalie. *Light and Enlightenment.* Cambridge: Cambridge University Press, 1957.

——. "Spinoza and the Early English Deists," *Journal of the History of Ideas,* Vol. 20 (January, 1959), pp. 23–46.

Collingwood, R. G. *The Idea of History.* New York: Oxford University Press, 1956.

Coser, L. A. *The Functions of Social Conflict.* Glencoe, Ill.: The Free Press, 1956.

Deane, Herbert A. *The Political and Social Ideas of St. Augustine.* New York: Columbia University Press, 1963.

Deborin, A. M. "Spinoza's World View," in *Spinoza in Soviet Philosophy.* Edited by George L. Kline. London: Routledge and Kegan Paul, 1952.

D'Entreves, A. P. *Natural Law.* New York: Harper and Row, 1965.

——. "Obeying Whom," *Political Studies,* Vol. XIII, No. 1 (February, 1965), pp. 1–14.

De la Court, Pieter. *The True Interest and Political Maxims of the Republic of Holland.* London: n. p., 1746.

Descartes, René. *Philosophical Works of Descartes.* 2 vols. New York: Dover, 1955.

DeVries, Peter. *The Mackerel Plaza.* New York: New American Library of World Literature, 1959.

Duff, Robert A. *Spinoza's Political and Ethical Philosophy.* Glasgow: James Maclehose and Sons, 1903.

Dunner, Joseph. *Baruch Spinoza and Western Democracy.* New York: Philosophical Library, 1955.

Eckstein, Walter. "Rousseau and Spinoza: Their Political Theories and Their Conception of Ethical Freedom," *Journal of the History of Ideas,* Vol. V, No. 3 (June, 1944), pp. 259–91.

Elwes, R. H. M. Introduction to *The Chief Works of Benedict de Spinoza.* 2 vols. New York: Dover, 1951.

Erikson, Erik. *Childhood and Society*, Second Edition. New York: W. W. Norton and Co., 1950.

Feuer, Lewis Samuel. *Spinoza and the Rise of Liberalism*. Boston: Beacon Press, 1958.

Froude, James Anthony. *Short Studies in Great Subjects: First Series*, Vol. I. London: Longmans, Green, and Co., 1895.

Geddes, James. *History of the Administration of John DeWitt*. The Hague: Martinus Nijhoff, 1879.

Geyl, Pieter. *The Netherlands in the Seventeenth Century*, Parts I and II. London: Ernest Benn, 1961.

Goldsmith, Maurice. *Hobbes's Science of Politics*. New York: Columbia University Press, 1966.

Gough, J. W. *The Social Contract*. Oxford: Clarendon Press, 1936.

Grabo, Carl. "Spinoza and Shelley," *The Chicago Jewish Forum*, Vol. I, No. 1 (Fall, 1942), pp. 43–50.

Green, T. H. *Lectures on the Principles of Political Obligation*. London: Longmans, 1941.

Halévy, Elie. *The Growth of Philosophic Radicalism*. Boston: Beacon Press, 1955.

Hallett, H. F. *Creation Emanation and Salvation*. The Hague: Martinus Nijhoff, 1962.

Hampshire, Stuart. *Spinoza*. Baltimore: Penguin, 1962.

———. Review of Wernham's translation *Benedict de Spinoza: The Political Works*. *The Philosophical Quarterly*, Vol. 9, No. 34 (January, 1959), pp. 80–83.

Hazard, Paul. *The European Mind*. Cleveland: World Publishing Co., 1963.

Hobbes, Thomas. *De Cive*. New York: Appleton-Century-Crofts, 1949.

———. *English Works*. 11 vols. Edited by Sir William Molesworth. London: John Bohn, 1840.

———. *Leviathan*. Edited by Michael Oakeshott. Oxford: Basil Blackwell, 1960.

Hubbeling, Hubertus Gezinus. *Spinoza's Methodology*. N. V. Groningen: Van Gorcum and Co., 1964.

Hume, David. *Political Essays*. Edited by Charles W. Hendel, New York: Liberal Arts Press, 1953.

——. *A Treatise of Human Nature*. Edited by L. A. Selby-Bigge. Oxford: Clarendon Press, 1888.

Jaffa, Harry V. "Comment on Oppenheim," *American Political Science Review*, Vol. 51 (March, 1957), pp. 54–64.

Janet, Paul. *Histoire de la Science Politique*, Vol. II. Paris: Alcan, 1913.

Kant, Immanuel. *Fundamental Principles of the Metaphysic of Morals*. New York: Liberal Arts Press, 1949.

——. *Perpetual Peace*. New York: Liberal Arts Press, 1948.

Kaufman, Walter A. *Nietzsche*. Princeton: Princeton University Press, 1950.

Kline, George L. *Spinoza in Soviet Philosophy*. London: Routledge and Kegan Paul, 1952.

Knight, Robert P. "Determinism, 'Freedom,' and Psychotherapy," in *Psychoanalytic Psychiatry and Psychology*. Edited by Robert P. Knight and C. R. Friedman. New York: International Universities Press, 1954.

Kohut, Heinz. "Introspection, Empathy, and Psychoanalysis," *Journal of the American Psychoanalytic Association*, Vol. VII, No. 3 (July, 1959), pp. 459–83.

Lefevre-Pontalis, Antonin. *John De Witt*. 2 vols. Translated by S. E. and A. Stephenson. London: Longmans, Green, and Co., 1885.

Lichtheim, George. *Marxism*. New York: Frederick A. Praeger, 1961.

Locke, John. *Two Treatises of Government*. Edited by Peter Laslett. New York: New American Library, 1965.

——. *Works*. London: Thomas Tegg, 1823.

Lucas, Jean. "The Life of the Late Mr. De Spinoza," in *The Oldest Biography of Spinoza*. Edited by A. Wolf. London: Allen and Unwin, 1927.

Luther, Martin. "Secular Authority," in *Martin Luther: Selections from His Writings*. Edited by John Dillenberger. New York: Doubleday and Co., 1961.

McKeon, Richard. *The Philosophy of Spinoza*. New York: Longmans, Green and Co., 1928.

Machiavelli, Niccolo. *The Discourses of Niccolo Machiavelli*. Edited by Leslie J. Walker. London: Routledge and Kegan Paul, 1950.

——. "The Prince," in *The Prince and the Discourses of Machiavelli*. New York: The Modern Library, 1940.

Marcuse, Herbert. *Eros and Civilization*. New York: Random House, 1962.

Martineau, James. *A Study of Spinoza*, Second Edition. London: Macmillan and Co., 1883.

——. *Types of Ethical Theory*, Third Edition, revised. Oxford: Clarendon Press, 1901.

Meerloo, Joost A. M. "Spinoza: A Look at His Psychological Concepts," *American Journal of Psychiatry*, Vol. 121, No. 9 (March, 1965), pp. 890–94.

Meinecke, Friederich. *Machiavellism*. New York: Praeger, 1965.

Metzger, Lore. "Coleridge's Vindication of Spinoza," *Journal of the History of Ideas*, Vol. XXI (April, 1960), pp. 279–93.

Mill, John Stuart. *On Liberty*. Indianapolis: Bobbs-Merrill, 1956.

Oakeshott, Michael. Introduction to *Leviathan* by Thomas Hobbes. Oxford: Blackwell, 1960.

Ogg, David. *Europe in the Seventeenth Century*, Eighth Edition. New York: Collier Books, 1962.

Parkinson, G. H. R. *Spinoza's Theory of Knowledge*. Oxford: Oxford University Press, 1954.

Plamenatz, John. *Man and Society*. 2 vols. London: Longmans, Green and Co., 1963.

Plato. *The Dialogues of Plato*. 2 vols. Translated by Benjamin Jowett. New York: Random House, 1937.

Pollock, Sir Frederick. *Spinoza: His Life and Philosophy*, Second Edition. New York: American Scholar Publications, 1966.

——. "Spinoza's Political Doctrine with Special Regard to His Relation to English Publicists," in *Chronicum Spinozarum*, Vol. I. The Hague: The Spinoza Society, 1921.

Polybius. *The Histories*. Edited by E. Badian. New York: Washington Square Press, 1966.

Pufendorf, Samuel. *De Jure Naturae et Gentium*. Translated by C. H. and W. A. Oldfather. Oxford: Clarendon Press, 1934.

Randall, J. H. *The Career of Philosophy*, Vol. I. New York: Columbia University Press, 1962.

Renier, G. J. *The Dutch Nation*. London: Allen and Unwin, 1944.

Richter, Gustav Theodor. *Spinoza's Philosophische Terminologie*. Leipzig: Barth, 1913.

Roth, Leon. *Spinoza*. Allen and Unwin, 1929.

——. *Spinoza, Descartes and Maimonides*. New York: Russell and Russell, 1963.

Rousseau, Jean-Jacques. *Emile*. New York: Everyman Library, 1911.

——. *Political Writings*. Translated and edited by Frederick Watkins. New York: Nelson, 1953.

——. *The Social Contract*. New York: Everyman Library, 1950.

Santayana, George. *Dominations and Powers*. New York: Scribner's, 1951.

——. Introduction to *Spinoza's Ethics and de Intellectus Emendatione*. London: J. M. Dent, 1910.

Saw, R. L. *A Vindication of Metaphysics*. London: Macmillan and Co., 1951.

Schöffer, Ivo. *A Short History of the Netherlands*. Amsterdam: Albert De Lange, 1956.

Simmel, George. *Conflict*. Glencoe, Ill.: The Free Press, 1956.

Smith, T. V. "Spinoza's Political and Moral Philosophy," in *Spinoza: The Man and His Thought*. Edited by Edward L. Schaub. Chicago: Open Court Publishing Co., 1933.

Sorel, George. *Reflections on Violence*. Glencoe, Ill.: The Free Press, 1950.

Spinoza, B. de. *Benedict de Spinoza: The Political Works*. Translated by A. G. Wernham. Oxford: Clarendon Press, 1958.

——. *The Chief Works of Benedict de Spinoza*. 2 vols. Translated by R. H. M. Elwes. New York: Dover Publications, 1951.

——. *The Correspondence of Spinoza*. Translated by A. Wolf. New York: Dial Press, 1927.

——. *The Principles of Descartes' Philosophy*. Translated by H. H. Britan. LaSalle, Ill.: Open Court Publishing Co., 1943.

——. *Spinoza, Opera*. 4 vols. Edited by Carl Gebhardt. Heidelberg: Carl Winters, 1925.

——. *Spinoza's Short Treatise on God, Man, and His Well-Being*. Translated by A. Wolf. New York: Russell and Russell, 1963.

Stephen, Leslie. *English Thought in the Eighteenth Century*. 3 vols. London: Smith, Elder and Co., 1902.

Strauss, Leo. *Spinoza's Critique of Religion*. New York: Schocken Books, 1965.

Temple, Sir William. *Works of Sir William Temple.* 4 vols. London: S. Hamilton, 1814.

Vaughan, C. E. *The Political Writings of Jean-Jacques Rousseau.* 2 vols. New York: John Wiley and Sons, 1962.

——. *Studies in the History of Political Philosophy.* 2 vols. New York: Russell and Russell, 1960.

Vlekke, Bernard H. M. *Evolution of the Dutch Nation.* New York: Roy Publishers, 1945.

Waelder, Robert. *Basic Theory of Psychoanalysis.* New York: International Universities Press, 1960.

——. "Psychic Determinism and the Possibility of Prediction," *Psychoanalytic Quarterly,* Vol. XXXII, No. 1 (1963), pp. 15–42.

Warrender, Howard. *The Political Philosophy of Hobbes.* Oxford: Oxford University Press, 1957.

Weber, Max. *From Max Weber: Essays in Sociology.* Edited by H. H. Gerth and C. W. Mills. New York: Oxford University Press, 1946.

Wernham, A. G. Introduction to *Benedict de Spinoza: The Political Works.* Oxford: Clarendon Press, 1958.

Wolf, A. *The Correspondence of Spinoza.* New York: Dial Press, 1927.

——. *A History of Science, Technology and Philosophy in the 16th and 17th Centuries.* 2 vols. New York: Harper and Brothers, 1959.

Wolfson, Harry A. *The Philosophy of Spinoza.* 2 vols. Cleveland: World Publishing Co., 1958.

Wolstein, Benjamin. "Romantic Spinoza in America," *Journal of the History of Ideas,* Vol. 14 (June, 1953), pp. 439–50.

Wood, Neal. Introduction to *The Art of War* by Niccolo Machiavelli. Indianapolis: Bobbs-Merrill, 1965.

Wrong, Dennis. "The Oversocialized Concept of Man in Modern Sociology," *The American Sociological Review,* Vol. XXVI, No. 2 (April, 1961), pp. 183–92.

Zac, Sylvain. *L'Idée de Vie dans la Philosophie de Spinoza.* Paris: Presses Universitaire de France, 1963.

Zumthor, Paul. *Daily Life in Rembrandt's Holland.* New York: Macmillan, 1963.

Index

❖